The Musician's Practice Companion
VOLUME I

PRACTICING FOR ARTISTIC SUCCESS

The Musician's Guide to Self-Empowerment

Burton Kaplan

 Perception Development Techniques, New York

Book design and typesetting by Quad Right, Inc., New York City
Illustrations by Elizabeth Hodes

For permissions, please contact Perception Development Techniques, 415 West Hill Road, Morris, NY 13808.
For ordering information, call 212-662-6634 or go to www.magicmountainmusic.org.

Printed in the United States
10 9 8 7 6 5 4

ISBN 10: 0-918316-05-7
ISBN 13: 978-0-918316-05-9

Also by Burton Kaplan

The Musician's Practice Log

A Rhythm Sight-Reader, Volumes 1 and 2

A Basic Skills Pitch Sight-Reader

TABLE OF CONTENTS

Acknowledgments

It was 1963. I had fallen precipitously in love with teaching and with my students, who were so trusting and willing to try whatever I showed them. But love is blind, and so was I, to the extraordinary adventure that awaited me. At each moment of insight, I thought I had the dragon by the tail. But much against my will, I discovered that I had much more to learn. I had to endure the pain of recognizing that applying what I learned about teaching was a totally different experience than trying to write it out for musicians and teachers whom I would never meet. I do not believe that I will ever stop improving the articulation of this knowledge. This book is my first major effort in that direction. Therefore, I am taking this occasion to thank all the students who put so much faith in my teaching and to acknowledge my debt to their devotion and determination to succeed. They range from the littlest, who at 5 and 6 years of age could not fathom where it all might lead, to the many professionals and pre-professionals who come to—and return to—Magic Mountain Music Farm for study that will advance their careers and refresh their artistic spirits. Over the years, I have been privileged to touch several thousand lives directly as a teacher, and I am grateful to you all.

Of course, along the way there have been a few musicians who have a unique ability to articulate this knowledge or who have extended the new practice pedagogy to others. Three musicians who use this practice pedagogy with children are Susan Crawford in Minneapolis, Eleanor Angel in Palo Alto, and Beatrice Stanley in Houston.

I would like to thank Richard Adams, Vice President and Dean of Faculty of Manhattan School of Music in New York City, for making space in the curriculum for my course, "Practicing for Artistic Success." I am indebted, as well, to Wilma Machover, a unique piano teacher and trainer of teachers, who saw merit in my work and arranged presentations and classes at the Hoff-Barthleson School in Scarsdale, NY. She also prompted me to foray into the international arena under the cloak of "Performance Power" to spread the word. Many people have facilitated Performance Power™ seminars all over the globe: Eleanor Angel, Valerie Dimond, Ralph Fielding, Linda Green, Hiroko Kagawa, Claudette Laureano, Susie Lee, Jeff Lerner, Stacey Lesartre, Mary McGeer, Ann Miklich, Thalia Moore, Katharine Rapoport, Ellen Sanders, Reed Smith, Beatrice Stanley, Beverley Spotton, Elizabeth Storm, Marvin Suson, Noralee Walker, Beth Warne, and Susan Waterbury. If I have left anyone out, please forgive me.

Two pianists provided invaluable help in tailoring parts of the book for keyboard players: Jackie Chew and Cullan Bryant. Above all, Marvin Suson and Scott Anderson stand out as invaluable in helping to develop this pedagogy. Marvin's faith in my guidance has never wavered, and he has persevered and improved with my methods over the past 10 years. I have gained valuable knowledge from his feedback. Scott (Principal Clarinet in the Honolulu Symphony) has an extraordinary sensitivity to instructional organization and clarity, as well as a unique ability to formulate ideas so they are easily understood. His devotion in reading and re-reading this manuscript to help refine its meaning and impact is greatly appreciated and has moved me deeply. I am deeply indebted, as well, to my editor, Joan Kocsis, for her ability to be critical and pragmatic without overriding my writing style.

Finally, there are my two children, Daniel and Emma, who have allowed me to teach them, thereby enabling me to review all my ideas as they apply from the beginning.

Thank you all.

HOW TO GET MORE FOR YOUR EFFORT

Music is an intuitive art. Practicing is a conscious managerial skill. To practice effectively the musician must be in touch with his or her intuitive artistic impulses and *at the same time* stand outside the process as a coach, making an endless series of conscious managerial decisions. Most musicians have never been taught the management skills they need to effectively coach their own practice.

Part One helps you to evolve a conscious awareness of how your mind and body can cooperate to achieve solid technical and musical control of your instrument. Based on the most current knowledge about how people learn, it offers specific exercises in the form of techniques and strategies to develop your concentration, reflexive control, performance consistency and confidence, imagination, and time-management skills. The chapters in Part One also give you practical ways of dealing with the thorny issues of impatience, frustration, boredom, conscience, and guilt. These methods enable you to replace counterproductive habits with effective new ones, thereby helping you to fulfill your technical and musical potential.

CHAPTER 1
What Counts as Practice?

If I spend 5 minutes reflecting on what I've been doing in my practicing, is that practicing? Or am I practicing only when I play my instrument? A commonsense answer to these questions can help musicians whose practice is dominated by an overbearing conscience. I have met many musicians who meticulously count as practice only the time when they are actually playing their instruments. If we submit this idea to calm, rational examination, it is clearly an unreasonable regimenting of behavior.

In fact, there are many different types of practice: warming up, preparing for a performance, learning a new piece of music or skill, maintaining control of a piece of music or skill, and listening to recordings of pieces you are studying, just to mention a few. Each type of practice requires a different style of time management. To manage your practice effectively, you need to set aside time to reflect and consciously consider your options. The time it takes to make your practice plan, for example, must be made a part of your practice or there will be no time available for it.

Imagine you are preparing for a performance that takes place in a week and you are planning to play through your performance several times during your practice. What should you do between each play-through? Should you start again as soon as possible? On the contrary, it makes sense to rest and reflect on the successes and failures of the preceding play-through before you proceed to the next one. One useful strategy would be to make a list of problem spots. You might decide to practice those spots mentally, if not physically, before the next play-through. That might take 3 minutes of reflection, or 15 or 30 minutes, depending on your evaluation of the last play-through.

Practice that consists mostly of continuous sound for long periods of time is unlikely to be productive. This chapter describes a dozen types of practicing and the style of time management appropriate for each.

Warming Up

Warming up is an aspect of practicing that deserves reexamination. I have encountered musicians who believe that they must warm up for over an hour to be ready to practice, and others who do not warm up at all. On average, musicians appear to spend 20 to 30 minutes warming up before they get to work. Although on some occasions that may be necessary, usually getting ready to practice does not require so much time for someone who is practicing 5 to 6 days a week. Some musicians have a routine that involves playing the same series of scales and arpeggios in the same order until the "ready-to-practice" message comes from inside. Although this may work to some degree, its tedium is mind numbing and inefficient.

There are three parts of your system you must warm up to get ready to practice effectively: (1) your body, (2) your musical spirit or feelings, and (3) your focused concentration.

1. To warm up your **body**, do easy aerobic exercise for 3 minutes. You can do jumping jacks, arm rolls, body twisting, and the like. The activity gets your blood flowing to your extremities, thus warming up those muscle groups. That's all it takes to get them ready to do the physical part of playing a musical instrument

2. To warm up your **spirit**, pay attention to the mood you're in. If you are practicing a piece for which that mood is appropriate, play it now, trying to express the mood as you play. That will help to connect your spirit to your warmed-up body.

However, if you are not in the mood to play any of the pieces you are currently studying, you have two options. You can improvise in your current mood and gradually segue into the mood of one of your current pieces. Or you can pick a piece you know well that's appropriate to your mood and just play through some of it to enjoy expressing the mood.

3. Most of the time, warming up your spirit will also warm up your **concentration.** Otherwise, a useful way to warm up your concentration is to set a performance goal that demands concentration. For example, play a scale, arpeggio, or etude that you are currently studying until it stops improving from just repeating it. Usually that will require a few repetitions. Then decide which feature of the sound is weakest (i.e., rhythm, tone, intonation, or phrasing). As you work to improve the feature you chose as weakest, you will find yourself becoming absorbed in the work (i.e., your body, spirit, and concentration will become coordinated and you will find that you are warmed up).

Learning New Repertoire

When musicians learn new repertoire, they are often asked to perfect the technical details before understanding or expressing the music. I have found that the musician who practices interpreting and expressing the music before polishing the details advances to the final, polished product much more rapidly than when the procedure is reversed.

During the first 2 weeks, practice primarily to become aware of and express the meaningful musical gestures implied by the notation. It is particularly important to decide beginnings and ends of phrases, as well as the peaks and troughs of intensity in each phrase, and to learn to express this awareness.

After 2 weeks, you can assume that you have done as well as you can at your current skill level. To polish the piece, you will actually be involved in extending your general skill level to produce a higher quality of playing. That should involve exercises and etudes, not just work on the piece itself. If you use the new piece alone to increase your quality control, you will get tired of it. If you

use etudes to improve your control, you can even put the new piece aside for several days, which can serve to keep it fresh for a long time.

Learning a New Skill

Learning a new skill is like raising a child. You must nurture it with appropriate respect for each stage of its evolution, but you will hurt its development if you have any expectation of how fast you will acquire control of the skill. Instead, you must exercise an attitude of disinterested curiosity while you concentrate on acquiring the new physical and auditory sensations involved. This book is all about how to develop that coordination in as objective and yet passionate a manner as possible. (To get a feel for what is involved, read the sections "The Technique of Success at Any Cost" and "The Technique of Intimacy," Chapter 5.)

Relearning Old Repertoire

It can be a wonderful experience to pick up a piece of music learned months ago. In the interim, as you practiced other works, you were growing in skill and musical awareness without necessarily being aware of it. As a result, when you pick up a piece you once knew, it often feels joyous and freeing because (1) the "old glove" fits better than before and (2) you play better and gain fresh insights as you study it again. If you let yourself grow into the old work as a musically expressive structure and do not worry the technique to death prematurely, you stand to gain significantly greater control than you had before.

Preparing for a Performance

"The Technique of the First Try" (Chapter 5) describes in detail a method of testing your performance readiness. If you are particularly interested in this feature of the book, skip to that section now to read about it.

Refining a Previously Learned Skill

Once you have practiced a new piece for 2 weeks, your control will stabilize at your current skill level. At this point, if you are not satisfied with that level at this time, your practice, becomes a matter of refining your skill. The guidelines for refining a previously learned skill are the subject of Chapter 5, which teaches the four steps of the Basic Work Process. Most musicians have virtually no training in this aspect of music practice, and their lack of knowledge causes pain and frustration that they endure for years. Chapter 5 is the heart of the first part of this book. If you take the time to develop the skills outlined in Chapter 5—the Techniques of Observation, Success at Any Cost, Intimacy, and the First Try—I guarantee that your practice will become a more meaningful, satisfying, and joyous experience.

Maintaining Control of a Piece of Music or a Skill

Once your control of a piece or skill is lodged in long-term memory (see "The Technique of Intimacy," Chapter 5), it does not require daily maintenance. Your control is then automatic and it seems to occur without your trying. Until that time, skipping a day of practice of a piece or skill increases the possibility of forgetting your recently acquired improvements. It is amazing how little you must practice to maintain your memory—once or twice through daily is enough. Therefore, if you have more to practice than fits comfortably in the time you currently have available, maintain control of the portion of your current repertoire you cannot cover by playing through it once or twice a day until you have the time available to do thorough work.

Taking Care of Your Body

During the past 40 years or so it has become increasingly accepted that playing a musical instrument should be treated as an athletic skill. During this time, we have seen the introduction of a new medical subspecialty, performing arts medicine, and problems like overuse syndrome and repetitive stress injury have become commonplace. These types of injuries occur in athletes, dancers, and musicians, as well as to those in office or factory occupations. Whether you type for

hours on a computer or play a musical instrument, the wear and tear on the soft tissues of the fingers, hand, wrist, and arm are similar from the point of view of athletic skill.

You must take care of your body if you expect it to perform optimally without breaking down. Preventive maintenance* is imperative; don't wait to be injured to take appropriate care of yourself. Be aware, however, that you will not find universal agreement about how to prevent injury. Take stretching, for example. Some people advise stretching before you start exercise or practice to avoid injury, while others advise stretching after exercise. An article in the *New York Times* about this issue reported that the most recent statistical evidence shows that stretching before exercise has no impact on avoiding injury. However, there is significant evidence that injury can be avoided or minimized by stretching *after* exercise.†

The amount and kind of effort you put into taking care of yourself depends on the characteristics of your own unique body, your drive to succeed, your stage of life, and the kind of training you have received.

If you must deal with many extra-musical, maintenance issues, you may be confronted with a significant practice time burden. Do not discount the management problem that results. If you need such maintenance on a regular basis, for whatever reason, treat it as a part of your practice. ***Set aside time during your practice to take care of it.*** Otherwise, it is unlikely you will find time during the rest of your day to maintain your system. And keep in mind that your "system" requires maintenance of your spirit as well as your body.

Getting Back into Shape

If you have stopped playing and practicing for 2 to 4 weeks or more, do not be surprised if you feel disconnected from your instrument. Some of the sensations musicians report include fingers feeling like rubber, tiring more quickly, not being able to support the sound as long as before, and poor timing.

---

*Several books and articles that can give you preventive maintenance guidance are Julie Lieberman, *You Are Your Instrument,* Huiksi Music, 1992; Jon Kabat-Zinn, *Wherever You Go, There You Are: Mindfulness Meditation in Everyday Life,* Hyperion, 1995; and Deborah Caplan, *Back Trouble,* Triad Publishing Co., 1987. In addition, several therapies are known to be helpful to musicians, including Alexander Technique, Feldenkrais, chiropractic, and massage therapy.

† Lorraine Kreahling, "New Thoughts about When Not to Stretch," *New York Times,* April 27, 2004.

Try to accept your plight and get back into playing gradually. The worst you can do is immediately try to play as much as you were playing before you stopped. Practice 30 to 60 minutes on the first day. Do not play anything that is at the limit of your skill. The next day, ask yourself how you feel as you start to play again. If the message from within is "I feel fine," add an additional interval of 30 to 60 minutes. If the message from within is "I feel tight," don't do any more than you did the day before.

This is particularly relevant if you have had a soft-tissue injury like tendonitis or overuse syndrome. If you have been treated by a physician for this type of injury and you are ready to practice again, the usual prescription is practice 5 minutes, rest 5 minutes. How long you continue this regimen depends on the extent of your injury.

Listening to Recordings of Pieces You Are Studying

Isn't it wonderful that we can buy numerous recordings by different artists of the works we are studying? Often we listen casually to these recordings while we dress, wash dishes, or do homework. Clearly, that is not a form of music practice. However, if you take the time to listen with focused concentration to understand a piece better, or to compare interpretations of different artists, then you are practicing. You cannot afford to go without touching your instrument for a day in favor of merely listening, but listening should be added to your practice schedule and pursued without guilt as long as it is purposeful. It is a good idea to position a listening session in your schedule so that it rests your body after a demanding round of intense playing.

Reading Books about Instrumental Technique and Musical Interpretation

Music is not often approached by reading books, but there are worthwhile books to guide your practice, give you insight into technique, and increase your interpretative ability (see "Books Related to Music Practice," p. 101). Other books provide valuable information on taking care of your body and mind in the practice room and on the stage (see Bibliography, p. 101). I recommend that you choose the material you read based on the needs that arise in your practice. As I suggested under "Listening to Recordings," schedule your reading so that it rests your body after a period of intense playing and count it as practice.

Planning Your Practice for Tomorrow

I recommend that you make your practice plan for tomorrow at the end of your practice today. Right after you finish your practice, you have the best memory of today's events and are therefore most capable of strategizing for tomorrow. If you conclude that you should follow the same plan as today, tomorrow's plan will take no time at all. But when you do need time to reflect on a possible change of plan for tomorrow, consider that part of your practice. Otherwise, where will the time come from to make your plan? For more on this subject, see Chapter 7, which describes specific ways of making your practice plan from day to day.

In short, anything you do to enhance your development as a musician or improve your playing counts as practice. If more musicians adopted this attitude, there would be fewer repetitive stress injuries, more insightful musicianship, and more meaningful and productive practicing.

CHAPTER 2
Using the Book to Guide Your Practice

Practicing for Artistic Success

If you were trying to become an Olympic athlete in any sport, you would be with your coach at least 5 days a week for years. Though she would not pay attention to you exclusively for every moment of each of those days, she would be available to answer questions and guide you daily. And if your talent appeared exceptional, you would earn more exclusive attention. That is an indication of the complexity of training your body and mind to coordinate for performance at levels that reach and extend human potential. Playing a musical instrument has the same sort of complexity. But most musicians receive, at best, an hour of coaching once a week during the school year and sometimes more during the summer.

On the basis of that hour, you are expected to guide your practice for 1 to 6 hours each day until you see your coach again. History tells us that some musicians are capable of achieving extraordinary results in the context of that limited contact with their coaches, although once you are showing that much promise, you get more frequent attention. Most musicians achieve little in comparison to their potential. In my experience, this stifled development is not for want of talent, but for want of the ability to effectively coach oneself. In other words, those who succeed are gifted at more than the obvious coordinated music-making ability; they are gifted at empowering themselves alone in the practice room, as well.

Unfortunately, the preceding analysis is not reflected in instrumental music pedagogy. I have heard many instrumental music teachers express the thought, "If only I could practice with my students every day for an hour, they would be able to play incredibly well." This kind of thinking should have led to the development of an elaborate pedagogy of practice, but that has not occurred. In spite of the obvious need for auxiliary courses in self-coaching to accompany all music lessons, the music community has shown no inclination to add such instruction to the curriculum at any level. This book introduces a pedagogy of practice. More importantly, it brings the knowledge directly to the musician.

Understanding Is Doing

There are two ideas you should keep in mind at all times as you use this self-empowerment guide to practicing: **Understanding is doing**, and **doing is understanding**. If you read this book and think, "Oh, I get it!" and put it aside, your practice will change very little. You will gain extensive knowledge, but it will not help you to practice more effectively unless you use your new understanding to change your behavior when you practice.

It is not simple to do this. Our practice spaces are private. We already have well-cultivated habits. Habits have a built-in resistance to change. In addition, you might easily be overwhelmed after reading just one chapter of this book with how much there is to know and how much there is to change. It is essential, therefore, that you have a method to help you transform this new knowledge into new actions.

Five Ways to Use the Book

You can enter this book from a number of avenues and get benefit from it. Five ways of tackling the information are shown below. Before going on, be sure you've read Chapter 1.

1. Choose from a List of Common Problems.

In the seminars and workshops I have conducted during the last 35 years, I have asked musicians to name their most irritating practicing problems. Following is a list of common dilemmas for which most musicians do not have adequate solutions. If you identify strongly with a particular dilemma, skip to the page indicated to read about how to solve the problem.

- "I played it perfectly just before I went on stage/ went into the audition/went into my lesson, but my performance let me down."
  Solution: Read "The Technique of the First Try" (Chapter 5, p. 43).

- "I often feel that I have to start over again each day."
  Solution: Read "The Technique of Intimacy" (Chapter 5, p. 39).

- "I don't know how to be productive once I've become frustrated."
  Solution: Read "Impatience as Practice Power" (Chapter 6, p. 49).

- "I cannot sustain my concentration. My mind wanders."
  Solution: Read "Your Concentration Is Your Best Friend, Even When It Lets You Down" (Chapter 5, p. 36).

- "Though I practice 3, 4, 5, or 6 hours daily, I never have enough time to cover everything."
  Solution: Read Chapter 7 (p. 51).

- "I can't find enough time to put in to achieve my ambition."
  Solution: Read "Using the Technique of Success at Any Cost to Improve Concentration and Control Expectations" (Chapter 5, p. 37), and all of Chapter 7.

- "I keep reaching the same level of proficiency, but I cannot find a way to get beyond it."
  Solution: Read "The Technique of Success at Any Cost" and "The Technique of Intimacy" (Chapter 5, pp. 35 and 39), and then search the Table of Contents for specific practice strategies that address your particular concern for proficiency.

- "I know what I want to achieve, but I don't know the steps to get there."
  Solution: Read Chapter 5, The Basic Work Process (p. 29), and then search the Table of Contents for specific strategies related to your technical problem.

2. Read the Book, Prioritize Strategies and Techniques to Try, Then Try One at a Time.

Read the entire book. When you see a strategy, tip, or technique you think might help you, put the number 1, 2, or 3 next to it. The number 1 means that you consider this item exceptionally relevant, 2 means that you consider it of some relevance, and 3 means that you consider it of little relevance. Make a list of all the strategies you marked with a 1. When you've finished reading through the book, review everything you checked and **pick one change** to try, the one that seems most important of all those you checked. If you find that this change is helpful, continue to use it and reflect on its value for a week. After a week, go on to try something else. If that does not help, try another.

3. Choose a Topic from the Table of Contents.

Look in the Table of Contents for a problem you need to solve and read about the strategies offered to solve it. If more than one strategy is offered for your problem, read through them all, but pick only one at a time to try. If the strategy you pick improves your practice, continue to use it for a week before proceeding to another. If it does not improve your practice, abandon it and look for another to try.

4. Jump in at Chapter 5, The Basic Work Process.

Just turn to Chapter 5 and begin your adventure there.

CHAPTER 3
The Six Myths of Instrumental Music Practice: Evaluation and Update

Most of us have been taught a few general ideas to guide our practice. I call them the Six Myths of Practicing. They are myths in that they tell a simple story about a complex activity.

Myth 1 Practice every day, even when you don't feel like it.

Myth 2 Continue to practice even when you are frustrated; eventually it will pay off.

Myth 3 Practice slowly.

Myth 4 Repeat a lot.

Myth 5 Use the metronome to improve your rhythm.

Myth 6 Isolate parts to improve them.

While these myths contain some truth, taking them literally or applying them inappropriately can be counterproductive. The advice they offer is too sketchy to deal with the complex decision-making process involved in effective music practice. Informed by this advice, most musicians waste an enormous amount of their practice time and often hurt themselves psychologically and physically in the process, because they fail more often than they succeed.

It is not obvious why these myths have served as the primary practice guide for all instrumentalists for many centuries, as they are less than adequate. Though I cannot explain why these myths have endured, I can say with great certainty that when musicians get together to scrutinize their practice habits and experiment with new ways of practicing, they are capable of extraordinary change and transformation.* Practicing can become a continuously rewarding and meaningful activity instead of a frustrating chore, thereby enabling musicians to conquer technical goliaths and achieve great artistry.

We will begin by looking at and answering some of the questions prompted by these myths.

Myth I: Practice every day, even when you don't feel like it.

Though there is some truth to this direction, it is equally true that extreme regularity is numbing. It is also true that all of us are susceptible to the vagaries of living: illness, dental problems, feeling tired, and so on. Sometimes when we don't feel like practicing, there may be good reason not to. Therefore, if you hold to such an uncompromising idea, you might not be able to achieve your goal and you will develop a sense of inadequacy and poor self-esteem as a result.

Question: Can I ever take a day off? How do I decide? Should I wait until I'm totally disgusted before I take a day off?

Answer: All training regimens to develop skills, whether athletic or mental, include rest as an important feature of a consistent schedule. Recent experiments show that less than 8 hours of sleep each day interferes profoundly with skill development.[†] "Rest to refresh," then, is an important training guide. You need to rest between intervals of work during a day. And you need to rest after a number of consecutive days of work.

It is important, therefore, to plan a day off from practice each week. Do not determine your day of rest by the degree of despair or frustration you are feeling. If you wait until you are discouraged, you

---

*For the past 19 years, I have conducted Practice Marathon Retreats for musicians at Magic Mountain Music Farm in upper New York State. In daily workshops and in private lessons, we have examined music practice and experimented with improving practice strategies and attitudes. This guide is a systematization of the information accumulated in those workshops. It enables any musician who is ready to change to take a giant step forward in practice effectiveness.

† Walker, Brakefield, Seidman, et al., "Sleep and the Time Course of Motor Skill Learning," 2003.

may have waited too long and you will probably need more than a day to recover. If you have been conditioned to believe that it is wrong to take a day off, you may feel guilty when you actually try it. Give it a try, however, and evaluate the results from the reality of your experience—and don't just try it one time. Take one day off per week for a month or two before you decide if it is of value to you.

Myth 2: Continue to practice even when you are frustrated; eventually it will pay off.

Should Sisyphus continue pushing the stone up the hill in the hope of making it to the summit, even though each of the last 10,000 times he neared the top, the stone rolled back down? It is obvious that the idea of "eventually" can reach the point of absurdity. Too many musicians have learned to tolerate that world of absurdity when they practice. Is it any wonder that despair creeps into our psyches when we face practice challenges?

Question: Is there a threshold of frustration beyond which I should not continue? Sometimes I feel like throwing my instrument out the window; is it useful to continue to practice even under those circumstances?

Answer: Frustration is caused by unfulfilled expectations. We have all been taught that we must learn to tolerate some degree of frustration in order to progress. That may well be a necessary condition of life. In the practice room, however, you can learn to respond to frustration by adjusting your expectations to what is possible. Until you have achieved an improvement, you have not improved. There is no way to accurately predict how long the effort to improve will take. Frustration, then, is a signal to which you should respond long before you reach your boiling point. In fact, as frustration increases, concentration diminishes. For an in-depth discussion of controlling concentration, see "The Technique of Success at Any Cost: Setting an Achievable Goal and Finding a Strategy to Reach It" (Chapter 5, p. 35).

I have found that the most common cause of frustration in the practice room is the tendency of musicians to try today to improve each phrase to perfection. The donkey in Figure 3-1 is striving toward a carrot that is always out of reach. Also notice that the carrot is too big to get his mouth around (he wants to bite off more than he can chew). This picture illustrates the musician who tries to reach perfection each day in spite of the daily evidence that improvement is a gradual process and perfection is unattainable.

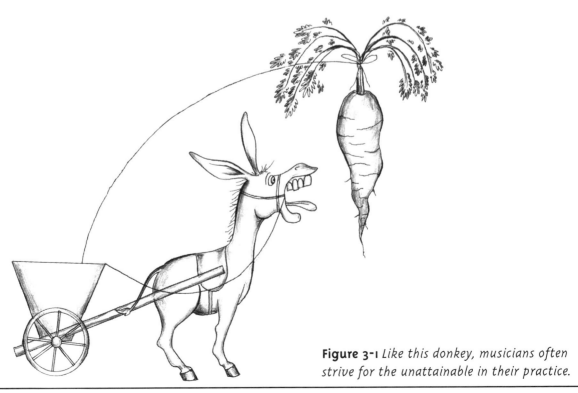

Figure 3-1 *Like this donkey, musicians often strive for the unattainable in their practice.*

Myth 3: Practice slowly.

Question: How do I know *how slowly* to play to improve?

Answer: You do not need a teacher to tell you how slowly to play to improve. There are internal signs you can easily identify to help you determine that tempo. The tempo you choose must fulfill all three of the following criteria: first, you should experience physical ease; second, you should feel calm; and third, you should be able to experience the notes as a musical pattern in slow motion.

Question: Is it possible to practice too slowly?

Answer: Yes! If you find that you are paying attention to each note separately instead of connecting them into a larger, musically meaningful pattern, you are playing too slowly. However, if for some reason you are compelled to play so slowly that it is either very difficult or impossible to experience a larger musical pattern, try the Note-Repetition Strategy (Chapter 12, p. 81). It will enable you to experience the pattern in spite of the slowness of the tempo.

Question: If I have practiced slowly, how do I know when to play at a tempo closer to the final tempo?

Answer: If you have practiced slowly for 2 or 3 days, and if you can maintain a steady pulse as you play *without stopping or hesitating*, then you are ready to play a little faster. The important judgment you must make is how much faster is "a little" faster?

Musicians often jump abruptly from their slow practice tempo to the final tempo. This is usually a mistake. In the excitement of experiencing the piece up to tempo, musicians gloss over errors while body tension and mental agitation increase.

To build your tempo from slow motion to performance tempo, first identify on the metronome the *current* tempo at which you have control. *Write the tempo down.* Be uncompromisingly honest in holding to a high standard of control at this slow tempo; you should feel calm and in command and meet all your expectations as to accuracy, beauty, and refinement. Then decide the metronome marking that corresponds to your final perform-

ance tempo and write that tempo down. As a general rule, divide the time between your "in control" tempo and your final performance tempo into four equal parts. Practice at each of those tempos as if they are steps on a ladder to approach the final performance tempo. Most musicians find it difficult to remember their practice tempos precisely from day to day. Always write down the tempos you practiced today, so you will be able to objectively evaluate your progress tomorrow.

Question: How important is it to practice musically when I practice slowly?

Answer: You can save yourself a lot of time and heartache if you practice musically when you practice slowly, with or without the metronome. *The coordinative timing of your body to express notes timed perfectly to the metronome beat is not the same as the timing that occurs when you play to inflect musically meaningful gestures.* There is a subtle but significant difference. When you express a musical idea, you create a rhythmic effect that has the power to move your audience. When you measure all your notes precisely with a metronome, you create a mechanical effect that lacks the power to communicate musical feeling. Mechanical timing and rhythmic timing are not the same (for an illustration, see under "Myth 5" later in the chapter). If you train your body movements to be mechanically in time *without* playing expressively, you will likely notice that your well-practiced coordination becomes unstable when you add musicality to the mix. If you train your body movements to express musical gestures from the start, you will not have to learn a different coordination later.

But beware: Playing expressively also has its pitfalls! When your primary purpose is to improve coordination, it is best to play with only 25% or 50% of your available emotional intensity. If you play with 100% emotional intensity before the improved coordination is stabilized, the excitement will cause your muscles to overwork. By modulating your emotional intensity without completely turning it off, your coordination will stabilize in the context of the rhythm of the final musical product and your muscular effort will not become distorted.

Myth 4: Repeat a lot.

Everyone seems to know that you must repeat a lot when you practice a musical instrument. In fact, in the nineteenth century, a word was used to refer to repetition during music practicing: "palinoia." It meant "to repeat over and over to perfect, as in practicing a musical instrument." This is not to be confused with paranoia, although excessive repetition could stem from fear or some pathological condition. When repetition is used as a tool rather than a panacea, it is meaningful and, at times, even pleasurable. The basic guidelines for useful and meaningful repetition follow.*

When Is Repetition Appropriate?

Question: How do I know when I should begin repeating?

Answer: There are five reasons to repeat when you practice:

1. Repeat to observe what is incorrect. If you were a painter, you might observe your painting for 5 or 10 minutes to determine what it needs to make it more correct or complete. As a musician, you have only an instant of time in which to determine the excellence of what you are hearing. Therefore, you must repeat the passage to further observe your work until you are certain of your perception and you can clearly articulate your observation. After one play-through, you may recognize that there was a flaw in what you heard, but you may not be able to pinpoint or determine what was the matter. So you play it again and yet again, until you are clear about what must be improved. For example, if you notice that a note is out of tune, you can only set a meaningful goal if (a) you know which note is out of tune; (b) you know whether the note is too sharp or too flat; and preferably, (c) you know the degree of sharpness or flatness.

2. Repeat to get progressively closer to your final goal. Once you have clarified what needs improvement, you need strategies to enable you to improve until you have formed the desired

result. This involves a three-step repetition: (1) imagine an improvement in a passage; (2) repeat the passage trying to achieve the improvement; (3) observe the result to determine if the improvement occurred. In item 1 (Repeat to observe what is incorrect), you would aim higher if the note was too flat and lower if the note was too sharp until you consistently decreased the range of error or until you achieved at least one success. This process of making successive approximations toward a goal is colloquially described as trial-and-error learning.

3. Repeat to lock in your recent success. In other words, repeat to develop a confident memory of an improvement. Your aim is to change the quality of control from requiring significant concentration to feeling automatic, *as if your body is doing it for you.* Therefore, when you repeat for this purpose, it is important that you only repeat a section that you would categorize as successful or improved. If, instead, you repeat a section that does not reflect the quality you want, you will create what I call "a perfect mistake." Whatever you play repeatedly during a period of 4 or 5 days will become an automatic, habituated part of your long-term memory, whether or not it is what you desire.

4. Repeat an entire work to determine its readiness for a performance. Test your ability to play through at a performance level on one try. See the "Technique of the First Try: Testing Performance Control" (Chapter 5, p. 43).

5. Repeat to maintain control of a work that is performance-ready. In order to maintain control of a work in which you have made a significant investment, repeat it at least once each day to maintain your current level of preparedness. When you return to it tomorrow or several days later, you will still have control.

Unfortunately, not all musicians make these five distinctions. Instead, they repeat spots, phrases, and sections in a palinoic manner, ad nauseam. This becomes a self-defeating experience, and does

---

* Dr. K. Anders Ericsson, University of Florida, has written extensively on repetition in music practice. One article of interest is K.A. Ericsson and N. Charness, "Expert Performance: Its Structure and Acquisition," *American Psychologist,* 1994, 49(8):725–747.

not lead to reliable control. Should control accidentally occur—and that does occasionally happen—the practicer has no way of knowing exactly which of the things he did created the desirable result. The next time a similar problem crops up, he must go through the same vague process with no guarantee of finding the solution.

When Is Repetition Inappropriate?

Question: Is it possible to repeat too much? What if, after 20 repetitions, I still play with little consistency or success?

Answer: Yes! It is possible to repeat too much. In general, you should know that if you have a very low percentage of success, such as 1 success in 15 tries, it means that your goal is too difficult (i.e., you are biting off more than you can chew). Revise your goal until you succeed with fewer repetitions.

In order to understand the useful limits of repetition in greater detail, turn now to "The Technique of Success at Any Cost: Setting an Achievable Goal and Finding a Strategy to Reach It" (Chapter 5, p. 35), "The Technique of Intimacy: Stabilizing the New Success" (Chapter 5, p. 39), and "The Rule of Impatience" (Chapter 6, p. 49).

Question: Should I repeat small groups of notes as many times as I repeat large sections?

Answer: Keep in mind that the phrase is the smallest meaningful unit of work. That does not mean that you should not isolate small musical gestures within a phrase to polish them, but you should isolate the small groups in order to increase the effectiveness of the expression of an entire phrase. If you increase your control of the small group without concern for how it integrates into the entire phrase, it is likely that the small group will create "lumps" or hesitations or simply break down when you play through the whole phrase in context.

When you isolate a small group of notes from a phrase to improve them, set a goal to repeat the improved version three times in a row. That is, if you have succeeded twice and you fail on the third try, you start again from zero. As soon as you have achieved three successes in a row, *immediately* try to integrate the improved small group back into the larger phrase.

Myth 5: Use the metronome to improve your rhythm.

Though music is an expression of emotion in sound, the emotion must be regulated by measuring it within a precisely timed beat. It seems paradoxical to time our emotional outpouring objectively. In life, when you express yourself, the timing or rhythm of your emotional expression varies with how you feel at the moment. The actual length of time you take to express yourself varies according to your circumstance and need, and it is not usually preplanned. In music, on the other hand, we must be prepared in advance to express specific feelings at particular moments in time and for particular amounts of time, as indicated in the score.

When emotion and time are exquisitely joined together in music, they cause a compelling rhythmic feeling in both the player and the listener. Many people think—incorrectly—that the musician who can play exactly in time to a metronomic pulse creates musical rhythm. But metronomic timing and rhythmic timing are not the same. When emotion expressed in sound is constrained within the "jail" of the metronomic beat, a subtle yet significant variation in timing occurs. It is like a war between the regulation of the metronomic beat and the abandon and expansiveness of the emotion. The result is what we refer to as *rhythmic timing*, in contrast to *mechanical timing*. Rhythm compels an audience to listen and want more; mechanical timing causes an audience to feel bored.

This idea of the seeming regularity of rhythm as contrasted with the absolute precision of the metronomic beat is not yet widely acknowledged in music pedagogy. I have tried to clarify it because I believe it helps the musician to understand when to use the metronome, and how to use it effectively. Figures 3-2 and 3-3 illustrate this point.

Question: How do I know when to use the metronome?

Answer: You need to use a metronome to guide your practice until you can play the part in time without it The downside of using a metronome is that musicians often sound more metronomic than musical when using one. This reveals a significant problem. The metronome measures objective time.

Figure 3-2 *Mozart wrote this music. Source: Mozart,* Sonata for Piano in C Major, *K545, Movement 1.*

Figure 3-3 *When an expert pianist played the music in Figure 3-2, it sounded like this.*

On the other hand, successful communication of musical expression requires that the musician interweave his emotional sensibility with his mathematically precise sense of time. When you stop using the metronome, your emotionality is more easily available to you, but it may make you lose control of the objective regularity of the beat. The aim of playing effectively with the metronome is to find a way to coordinate these two aspects, the objective and the subjective.

When you have one of the experiences listed below, you need to use a metronome as a tool to increase your control of objective musical timing:

• When you are playing at a slower tempo than the final tempo and you find or are told that you are dragging or rushing, use the metronome as a guide.

• When you have a tendency to rush any part of a work, use the metronome as a guide.

• When you want to figure out how to include the passion you feel in a certain part without altering the regularity of the beat, use the metronome as a guide.

There is a simple strategy you can use to determine whether or not you need to use the metronome. Record yourself playing without using the metronome. When you listen to the replay, turn on the metronome to find out how closely the recorded beat and the metronome beat coincide. In most instances, if you observe that you lose a beat or more within a phrase, then you should use the metronome until the same test shows that you are playing within the boundary of the metronomic beat.

Question: Is it a good strategy to start very slowly and increase the tempo one notch at a time?

Answer: This timeworn strategy is quite inefficient. When you proceed one notch at a time, the difference in difficulty is usually trivial. In order to experience a meaningful challenge and use your time efficiently, follow the guidelines shown in "The Basic Metronome Strategy" (Chapter 9, p. 66).

Myth 6: Isolate parts to improve them.

Musicians are easily overwhelmed by the number of details contained in just one phrase of music. Therefore, it is natural to reduce the number of details in order to pay greater attention to a few. However, as was the case with Myths 1 through 5, several questions present themselves to the musician who is trying to pursue this strategy of isolation.

Question: How do I decide what aspect of the music to work on?

Answer: At any given time during your practice, you will perceive many details to fix. There will likely be several aspects of the music or your playing that you could address. It is important that you do not make arbitrary choices as to what you work on. Instead, look for the *patterns of error* in what you hear. First, decide which of the following "categories" is weakest in your product: intonation, tone, rhythm, or expression. Always start by improving the weakest category first. (For a detailed description of this strategy, see "The Technique of Observation," Chapter 5, p. 29). Incidentally, when you work in this way, some of the other problems you perceive will resolve themselves without your directly addressing them.

Question: What criteria should I use to decide how small a section of the music to isolate?

Answer: The number of notes or size of the musical gesture you isolate should be related to the difficulty of improving them, as follows: Taking 30 minutes to stabilize the pitch of two notes is too inefficient to be useful. Therefore, one criterion is that *it should not take more than 5 minutes to improve a small section or group of notes.* If it does, make the goal less demanding.

Another criterion to consider is the limitations of your current knowledge and ability to achieve a particular level of quality. In your effort to make an improvement, you have a choice between two kinds of practice: (1) Practice to increase your sen-

sitivity so that you can achieve a new level of precision, or (2) use your already available sensitivity to create better musical gestures. To elaborate further:

1. If you do not yet have the pitch sensitivity or the rhythmic sensitivity needed to improve a musical gesture, there is no point in working on the entire musical gesture. In the instance of pitch sensitivity, a string or wind player might first try to increase his sensitivity to the specific notes involved before putting them together to form an entire musical gesture. Now consider, how sensitive is sensitive enough? In a musical context, notes often go by so quickly that if you cannot perceive them accurately within a fiftieth of a second, you cannot expect to be able to control them. Musicians often mistakenly assume that, when they have played the notes in tune a few times slowly, they will be able to play them in tune at any speed, in any context. Such unrealistic expectations often lead to inordinate frustration, poor concentration, and lack of confidence. When you first isolate a note and listen to it long and carefully to determine its accuracy, do not expect that this work alone will be enough to fix your problem when you play the entire phrase at tempo. All instrumentalists must develop an equivalent hypersensitivity in their perception of rhythm and tone, as well as expression.

You must practice until you have developed what is at first a barely perceptible awareness into an extreme sensitivity. When you believe that you have developed such hypersensitivity, put it to the test by playing a whole phrase that demands this awareness. Then stop and ask yourself if you actually heard the improvement. If you cannot tell, then you are not yet sensitive enough. If you are certain of what you have heard, you are ready to integrate the detail into the larger context.

2. When you are using your already available sensitivity to form the phrase, again, it is best to isolate patterns of notes that form musical gestures rather than individual notes or arbitrary groups of notes. To clarify what this means, look at Figure 3-4. Example "a" shows the phrase as written. In example "b," the brackets indicate the smallest meaningful musical gestures. In example "c," the brackets show sub-units that are not "musical gestures" but are rhythmic sub-groups that must be linked together (as in example "b") in order to be meaningful. Most of the time, if you try to express rhythmic sub-groups rather than musical gestures, your coordination will suffer.

Question: How large a group of notes is too large to isolate?

Answer: Musicians have a tendency to bite off more than they can chew when they practice. The issue is less how large a group is too large than how long it will take to fix what is wrong. There are always time constraints in practicing, and musicians characteristically allow themselves to be guided by unconscious expectations instead of consciously managing their work according to the known time constraints.

It is of great importance to protect yourself from the trap of unreasonable expectations when you practice. A strategy that will help you is to set your goals to *improve* rather than to *perfect*. Aim to *decrease the range of error* rather than to create perfection. If each day you decrease the range of error in any part of your playing, after 10 or 20 days you will most likely have achieved perfection without trying to control it directly. This strategy will lead you to feel pride and confidence in your work. It will protect you from becoming unduly frustrated. For a detailed understanding of decreasing the range of error to solve a problem and a technique to stabilize control of gradual improvements, see "The Technique of Success at Any Cost" and "The Technique of Intimacy" (Chapter 5, pp. 35 and 39).

Question: Why is it that, after I've isolated and perfected several sections out of context, I can't always control them as well in context?

Answer: This is the ultimate dilemma musicians face when they practice. Many have learned to live with this fact of practice life—grin and bear it, so

Figure 3-4

to speak—because a certain amount of contextual integration eventually occurs. I am happy to report that there is a specific strategy to help you control the integration of work on details into the continuous flow of the music (see "The Isolation-Integration Strategy," Chapter 9, p. 62).

Reviewing the Six Myths of Practicing

The evaluation and update of the six myths of practicing have revealed a lot of information that can help a musician practice more efficiently. So far, the answers to the questions stimulated by the simplistic practice myths that are our heritage lead to saving time, muscular effort, and psychological torment. The references to later parts of the text attest to how much more knowledge is to come. You can look forward to much more improvement in efficiency and pleasure as you apply the strategies illustrated in the rest of this book.

Moving Beyond the Myths

Effective practice is a skill of informed management. Each time you stop because you have just failed (or succeeded!) in achieving a goal, you need to "manage" what to do next. To make appropriate managerial decisions, you need to understand how the human system acquires skill behaviorally, neurologically, and physiologically—how we learn. As you apply the principles for making effective decisions, you will also gain the power to create new ways to reach your goals and experience enhanced motivation to practice. Armed with these answers to the questions raised by the Six Myths of Practicing, you are already better equipped to practice more effectively. These answers, however, are only a beginning; read on! Be assured that, although the process is complex, what you have yet to learn as you deepen your understanding is fascinating and will ultimately lead you to much greater fulfillment as a musician.

CHAPTER 4

The Third Hand:
The Source of Control

Successful performance of instrumental music depends on coordination. Most often, we study the coordination of the left and right hands, arms, and fingers and, for wind instrumentalists, the embouchure, oral cavity, and breathing mechanism. Coordination also involves the eyes when reading music. The excellence of overall coordination depends on the rhythmic timing of the body movements, as specified in the musical score.

Less obviously, the mind, though physically intangible, is an essential part of this timing process. I have found it pedagogically useful to conceive of the mind as a *Third Hand*. I think of the mind as a hand because *the thought process must be timed as precisely as the left and right hands* to create music using an instrument. Ultimately, the developing musician can be empowered to achieve confident performance control by understanding how to manipulate the Third Hand to improve coordination.

Training the Third Hand to Develop the Instrumental Gymnast: Reflexive Control

Your mind organizes and maintains the coordination of your body when you play your instrument. The mind can be compared to a toolbox. The tools include imaging, observing, evaluating, guessing, hypothesizing, planning, directing, and feeling. These tools are like the fingers of your Third Hand. It is important that you use the appropriate tool to create the desired result.

For instrumentalists one of the most important mental tools is imaging. In our lives, we image constantly in order to move and communicate. Imaging is so seamlessly interwoven into our experience that most of the time we are unaware that we are using it to control our behavior. (See

Chapter 8 for a detailed discussion of imaging as a strategy to increase control.) To become more conscious of imaging in your experience, try this exercise.

1. Start by sitting in a chair.

2. Count to 5 in your mind, slowly. When you reach the number 5, suddenly raise your left arm straight into the air and get up and walk across the room quickly, keeping your left arm up.

3. Touch the far wall with your right hand. Immediately turn around, walk quickly back to your chair, and sit down.

4. When seated, put your left arm down.

Now, review your experience. In order to guide your actions according to the specified instructions, you had to form an image of what to do *before* you moved. You could not have acted in the specified way if the image did not precede the action. Your imaging mind "told" your body what to do.

If it were important to learn this sequence of actions to the point of reflexive control, as in playing a musical instrument, you would practice it until your actions became reflexive. *Reflexive control* involves performing a sequence of actions without conscious awareness of the imaging process guiding the actions.

When you first learned to play your instrument, you had to use your imaging capacity in the same conscious way you followed the directions above. In order to continue to improve, regardless of your playing level, you must continue to form images. You use imaging first to learn the sequences of notes in a new piece and second, to refine the gestures and sounds that bring the piece to life. As you play a newly studied piece over and over, you become less conscious of the images that helped give you control, and your control becomes increasingly reflexive or "mindless." It is possible for the reflexive control to be so well conditioned that you can engage in some other activity, such as watching TV or carrying on a conversation, at the same time you play a piece you know.

Reflexive control is commonly described by the expression "the mind is in the fingers." The instrumental gymnast flourishes in this state of mindless control, but keep in mind that this state does not guarantee musical expression or communication. When there is so much room in the mind that little conscious mindfulness is required to sustain gymnastic control, the musician has significant free conscious mental attention available to communicate her expressive musical ideas. It is at this stage of reflexive technical control that the musician has a chance to become a compelling musical artist. Too often, musicians are satisfied with being only instrumental gymnasts.

Training the Third Hand to Develop the Musical Artist

Music as artistic communication is difficult to talk about. We cannot say what it is, but we know when we experience it. It compels us to listen, and we find ourselves paying such complete attention that ordinary cares and worries recede into the background.

Most current pedagogy does not take into account the internal workings of the mind that enable us to create a compelling performance. The idea of the mind as the Third Hand gives us a pragmatic way to conceptualize this mechanism. When the mind coordinates gymnastic timing and expressive timing, the audience is compelled to listen. This coordination involves a unique manipulation of the mind's capacity to image, observe, evaluate, and feel. Here is how the coordination works.

1. **Imagine a "musical idea"** that you consider compelling. To affect an audience positively, the image must have an emotional character and be conceived within the constraints of rhythm, pitch, and musical dynamics, as indicated in the score.

2. **Before you begin to play**, imagine the sound of the musical idea you wish to express. It makes sense to think of this imagined sound as "the anticipated future."

3. **As you play** you must continually observe whether the sound you are hearing matches the sound you imagined a moment before—the anticipated future. (It seems self-evident that you must imagine the sound before you can move to express it.) Because music is constrained by a regular rhythmic pulse, the relationship between the anticipated future and the movements necessary to create the sound must be rhythmic and precise. Figure 4-1 shows how the imagined sound (the anticipated future) coordinates with the sound that emerges from your instrument.

4. **If you are practicing and you observe that the sound you hear as you play does not correspond precisely to the sound you imagined,** stop to evaluate what's going wrong and try again. When you try again, you will succeed only if your analysis of the problem(s) preventing the coordination of your Third Hand and your body are correct. If you do not include your Third Hand in your analysis, you may never solve the problem at all.

Some possible problems in coordinating well include these:

- The sound image in your Third Hand has flaws in rhythm, intonation, tone, phrasing, or style. See Chapter 8 (p. 57) to understand this kind of problem.

- The sound image in your Third Hand needs to be more detailed, precise, or vivid.

- The sound image in your Third Hand is too far ahead of your playing actions.

- The sound image in your Third Hand occurs after your body has already moved to make the sound.

If you are performing and you observe that the sound you hear is not the sound you imagined, you cannot stop and fix what has already gone by. Therefore, when you are practicing and the sound

Figure 4-1 *Notice that the imagined sound (anticipated future), "b," occurs slightly after the written music is read, "a." The sound "c" that emerges from your instrument occurs after "a" and "b" have occurred. This coordination must be continued, as shown, if the musician is to continue to express his musical ideas seamlessly, without interruption. Source: Mendelssohn,* Violin Concerto in E Minor.

you hear is not the sound you imagined, stop and correct it. Then repeat the desired experience so that you train your Third Hand to always imagine the sound you want to hear in advance of the movements of your body.

A Language Model for Mind-Body Coordination When Playing a Musical Instrument

If you are not used to thinking about how your Third Hand coordinates with your body when you play, the description above probably seems either formidable or nonsense. Fortunately, however, we each have a similar experience of image, movement, and sound when we converse. You may never have considered the mechanism by which

thought is coordinated with speech. Unlike the mind-body coordination necessary for making music, you don't have to design the relationship between your thoughts and your voice in order to speak because it is genetically given.*

To become aware of the coordination of image and movement in speaking, try this: As you speak, pay attention to *the moment* you conceive the thought that you hear coming out of your mouth. It will feel awkward to examine the process as you participate in it, but it is possible. You will notice that you experience the thought *before* you speak. Notice as well that the image of what you plan to say (i.e., the anticipated future) contains both words and the expressive ("felt") inflection of those words, which is also a part of your expression.

*Pinker, *The Language Instinct.*

The timing of thought, speech, and feeling when you speak fluently is exquisitely coordinated. It is a genetic gift. There is a continual overlap between the expressive thought you are about to give birth to as sound and gesture (the anticipated future), the validation of the expressed thought as representing what you mean (the present), and the awareness of the impact of that thought on the person you're addressing (which could stimulate you to alter the style and content of your presentation). In other words, if you have a lot to say, you will notice that the next thought comes into your head before you finish expressing the preceding thought.

In playing or singing music, the process is virtually the same, with one important difference: The rhythm of conversational speech is not measured in regular beats, the way we measure time in music. For the musician to communicate effectively to her audience, the same relationship of imagined sound, evaluated sound, and overlapping imaging of the next sound must be designed and conditioned. This image-to-sound process must take place within the constraints of the printed music (rhythm, pitch, etc.). This process is not inborn; it must be learned.

This description of the coordinative mechanism underlying effective musical performance sheds light on a common and disconcerting musical experience. Have you ever felt deeply connected to your musical expression as you perform, only to find that the audience was not moved by your performance? It can be a devastating experience.

Using the concept of a three-handed coordination, this experience is both comprehensible and capable of improvement. A player who has not imaged the desired sound *before* starting to play may still be experiencing her musical expression within, but too late to coordinate with the conditioned reflexive body movements for the image to be reflected in the actual sound. When that happens, the "finger" of the Third Hand that controls the musical image is moving *behind* the playing parts of the body and therefore cannot influence those parts to create the subtle variations of gesture necessary to express the musical image. In other words, the imaging finger of the Third Hand is not coordinated with the fingers of the left and right hand and/or the tongue and breathing apparatus. The audience will not, therefore, hear the player's musical thoughts, though the player is earnestly trying to convey them.

Coordinating the Third Hand to Manage Your Practice Effectively

Music is an intuitive art. Practicing is a conscious managerial skill. To practice effectively the musician must be in touch with her intuitive artistic impulses, and *simultaneously* stand outside the process as a coach, making an endless series of conscious managerial decisions, or micromanaging. These decisions include evaluating the work's performance readiness, estimating a set of sub-goals for today to bring her closer to performance readiness tomorrow, choosing appropriate strategies to achieve the sub-goals, deciding how much material to repeat and when and how often to repeat it, and so on.

Unfortunately, music pedagogy does not yet offer a methodical system for musicians to maximize their practice efforts. A number of books about music practice have appeared in the last 20 years (see the Appendix), but their effect on music pedagogy, as well as the evolving musician, both amateur and professional, is still not appreciable. To my knowledge, no books address the issue of self-coaching in a systematic way. I have found that musicians at the top of the profession have all worked out managerial systems for themselves, but none of them have made their management styles into a systematic pedagogy. This book attempts to do just that.

CHAPTER 5
The Basic Work Process

> *Making music is an intuitive process. To improve intuitive functioning we bring to consciousness sub-processes of the whole and consciously manage their refinement. Then we reinsert them into the intuitive whole.*

To improve your mastery of a particular musical or technical event efficiently, you must guide your practice through a series of specific, practical steps. I call these steps the Basic Work Process. There are four sequential techniques in the Basic Work Process: the Technique of Observation, the Technique of Success at Any Cost, the Technique of Intimacy, and the Technique of the First Try.

They are techniques in the same sense that your ability to produce a tone on your instrument is a technique. They require practice and repetition to be fully mastered. The more experienced you are with these techniques, the more you will benefit. The four techniques will help you coach yourself effectively when you practice. When you have mastered the techniques of the Basic Work Process, you will be able to identify the most appropriate problem to solve next, choose a strategy to solve the problem, and stabilize the result so that you have consistent control when you perform.

In addition to improving practice efficiency, these four techniques will help you avoid the most bothersome impediments to progress that plague all musicians when they practice: frustration, boredom, despair, self-doubt, and self-deprecation. You might even experience joy, pleasure, and satisfaction instead.

Keep in mind that you can already play your instrument with some skill, and that without exposure to these techniques you have already made many improvements in your playing. However, you may seldom know precisely which practice activity caused those improvements. I can say with certainty that when you have improved during practice, you must have employed one of these techniques, whether or not you were conscious that you were doing so.

As you gain an understanding of the techniques, you will acquire the ability to consciously coach yourself to control improvement from day to day. But be aware! In a performance art, **understanding is doing**. For the Basic Work Process to become a *reflexive*, *habitual* part of your practice behavior, you must exercise your ability to use each technique, first separately and then in sequence (i.e., in the order described above). Otherwise, your *understanding* will lie stillborn in your mind, incapable of improving your practice. The "To Understand" section describes each technique. A section called "Practicing the Technique of . . ." details the steps required to develop mastery of the technique. Study all the steps within each technique *by actually doing them*, as you would practice an instrumental etude. Repeat each technique to become aware of its value in your practicing and to be able to use it when it is the perfect tool to help you improve your playing.

1 The Technique of Observation: Identifying and Prioritizing Problems

To Understand

To solve a problem you must notice that it exists. For example, you cannot improve the tuning of a note if you have not observed that it is out of tune. What is less obvious, however, is that you cannot correct an out-of-tune note with certainty until you have observed whether it is too sharp or too flat. Once you have observed that a note is sharp, for example, you can direct yourself to make it flatter. Otherwise, your chances of success are at best 50-50, and because of that uncertainty, you will be plagued with anxiety.

This principle applies to solving all music practice problems: *To increase your control of a skill, you must first observe what is out of control to gather appropriate objective information about it.* You will then be armed with information that can enable you to improve your control.

One of the tools in the toolbox of your mind ("Training the Third Hand to Develop the Instrumental Gymnast," Chapter 4, p. 25) is your capacity to observe. In this manual, I will refer to your observing mind as your Observer. Your Observer is one of the "fingers" of your Third Hand (see Chapter 4). If you learn how to exploit your Observer effectively, your productivity in practicing will increase dramatically.

Because we depend on our ability to observe at every instant of our lives, we take this capacity for granted. Most of the time, it functions below the level of conscious awareness. Perhaps that is why observation is not explicitly described in music pedagogy. However, it is of such paramount importance as a tool in developing skill that I will examine it in detail to explain how to use it effectively in music practicing.

Observation and Human Behavior

Awake or asleep, the observing quality of our mind (a "finger" of our Third Hand) is helping us to coordinate our internal and external environment to maintain our well-being. Most of the time, we are not conscious of its effort.

In waking life, for example, imagine taking a walk in the woods with a friend. The terrain is uneven, often unfamiliar. Nonetheless, you can carry on a conversation for long periods without tripping. You don't pay much attention to this miracle of control because it requires minimal conscious awareness and it works flawlessly. While you carry on your conversation, your Observer pays continual attention to the terrain, sometimes unconsciously, and sometimes prodded into partial consciousness by unique variations in the path. You automatically notice what is ahead to anticipate any variations in your movement that will be needed to negotiate the terrain while you continue your conversation. On the other hand, should you see a large boulder blocking your path ahead, you are likely to interrupt your conversation in order to negotiate a way around it. In other words,

you bring your observations to consciousness in order to describe the problem and solve it.

Likewise, when you are practicing, you must first acknowledge when your control is inadequate to achieve your desired performance level. Then you must **step outside the intuitive music-making mode** to make room to consciously coach yourself—to articulate the problems and use appropriate strategies to solve them. The Technique of Observation opens the door to evolving your internal practice coach to a new level of control.

Developing Your Conscious Observer

The Technique of Observation consists of two parts: the Pie Strategy and the Berry Strategy. These strategies enable you to hone your skill as an observer in the same way that you hone your instrumental skill when you practice scales and etudes. As with scales and etudes, you must exercise your Observer each day to keep it in shape. As your Observer becomes more objective and astute, your effectiveness in coaching yourself will increase significantly.

The Pie Strategy

Imagine that you are practicing and you feel that you are not progressing. You seem to have hit a wall. This is the moment when you wish you could go to your teacher and ask "What should I do next?" The Pie Strategy will empower you to answer that question objectively, *on your own*. The pie we're talking about looks like the one in Figure 5-1. The Pie Strategy enables you to take your

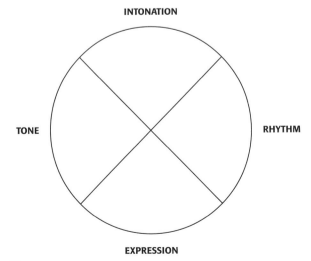

Figure 5-1

Pie A

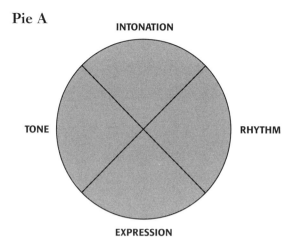

Pie B

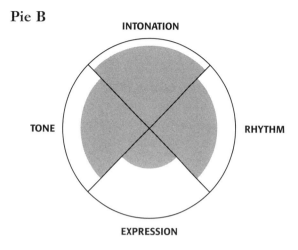

Pie C

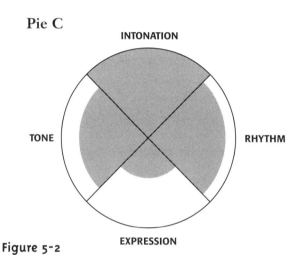

Pie D

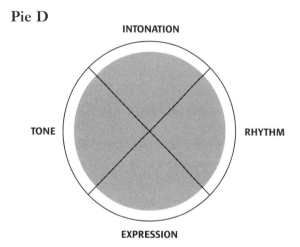

Figure 5-2

Observer out of your mental toolbox and put it at the center of your attention. Before I describe the steps of the strategy, I will describe the concept of the pie in more detail.

The main purpose of the Pie Strategy is to decide *what feature of the music to work on next*: tone, rhythm, intonation, or expression. Musicians often choose reflexively what they have been most sensitized to without giving it much thought. In string playing, for example, intonation tends to be the favorite. These reflexive decisions can easily lead us astray, as an examination of the "pies" in Figure 5-2 will show.

Pie A represents a superior performance. Pie B represents a stage of work when the practicer is considering what to do next. Should this practicer next improve the strongest slice, the weakest, or one in between? Pie C shows that the practicer chose to improve the intonation, which in Pie B was already the strongest. Pie D shows that the

practicer chose to improve the expression, which in Pie B was the weakest. It is likely that an average audience will appreciate the Pie D performance more than the Pie C performance. Since excellence invites comparison, the extreme disparity between the excellence of intonation in the Pie C performance and the other aspects of the sound will be particularly irritating. The balanced quality of the Pie D performance will be more satisfying. Therefore, *the primary aim of the Pie Strategy is to identify the weakest slice of the pie as the next quality to improve.*

There is a still more important reason to adopt this value system. In truth, these four aspects of your playing—these "slices" of the pie—cannot truly be separated from each other; in the musical context, they overlap. Intonation is profoundly affected by the quality of tone, rhythm, and expression; tone is equally affected by the quality of intonation, rhythm, and expression; and expression is obviously affected by rhythm, tone, and intonation. We artificially separate them for the convenience of narrowing our focus to improve our control of a single feature of the music at a time. We would easily be overwhelmed by trying to work on everything at once. Therefore, when you work to improve the quality of the weakest slice of the pie, there is usually a positive effect on the other slices and hence on the entire performance. Your overall control is likely to improve. Conversely, if you work on the strongest slice to make it stronger, the weakest will seem even weaker; you distort even your own perception of the wholeness of the musical product.

To use the Pie Strategy, follow the procedure below after warming up the passage:

Step 1 Say *out loud,* "I am going to play from _____ to _____ and observe for the strongest and weakest slices of the pie." **You must specify the exact beginning and ending of the excerpt you have chosen.**

Step 2 Play the amount you described. *You may not stop playing until you have finished the excerpt you specified.* In other words, **do not practice it.** Just observe for the qualities you specified. If you do stop for any reason, repeat Step 1 again. *As you play the passage,* continue to observe first, which of the four slices is strongest, and second, which is weakest. Make your observations while you are playing, not afterward. If observing the qualities of your sound *as you are playing* is not your habit, expect it to take many trials until you develop this ability.

Step 3 Within 10 seconds after you have stopped playing, complete the following statement by saying out loud, *without hesitation,* "I observed that the strongest slice was _____ and the weakest slice was _____." If it takes you longer than 10 seconds to begin expressing your observation, you did not make your observation while you were playing. Instead, you are replaying the phrase in memory and trying to observe what occurred after the event. This is contrary to the spirit of the task. *You must make your observations only as you play.* Begin again at Step 1.

Step 4 Write down your observations, like this:

Strongest	Weakest

Always make your observation of the strongest slice *before* making your observation of the weakest slice. When we are preoccupied only with what is wrong, we do not play as well as we can. By observing for both strongest and weakest features of your playing you will play as well as you can, in spite of whatever is weak.

Step 5 Observe the same phrase or section five times in a row. Each time, say aloud what you will do before playing as you follow Steps 1 through 4. Your aim is to identify *a pattern* of weakness. When one slice is identified as weakest three times out of five, as in Pattern A in Figure 5-3, you have identified a *pattern of weakness.* You are then ready to go on to the Berry Strategy. But what if the results are not decisive, as in Patterns B and C in Figure 5-3? In Pattern B, there is a tie for weakest slice between R and I, and in Pattern C, the responses seem to be random.

Pattern A (T [tone] = 3 for 5)		Pattern B (a tie between R & I)		Pattern C (no pattern emerges)	
S	**W**	**S**	**W**	**S**	**W**
I	T	T	I	T	I
I	R	I	R	I	E
R	T	R	I	E	R
E	R	I	R	R	T
I	T	E	T	T	I

Figure 5-3

Interpreting Your Results

Though the results are not always decisive, they are always meaningful. Patterns B and C each reveal something important about the practicer and the mental process that occurs when a musician uses the pie strategy.

Notice that in each of the three patterns, the weakest slice in one observation often becomes the strongest in the next. Indeed, a happy and frequent by-product of the Pie Strategy is that merely applying the strategy to a problem often solves it. These extraordinary effects have an important explanation. ***In order for musicians to determine the relative strength and weakness of each slice of the pie, they must be referring their decision to an image of the music as a whole.*** Therefore, there is an unstated but ever-present holistic frame of reference within which to adjust the slices of the pie. A musician who can adjust the imbalance he just observed will try to improve it, though he continues to observe as his primary purpose. This manipulation appears to be relatively unconscious, a "trying without really trying." In biofeedback training this is referred to as *passive volition*. The aphorism "forewarned is forearmed" applies here.

It is interesting that most musicians ask, when making their first Pie Strategy observations, "Should I try to fix it?" The answer is, "You can do whatever you please as long as you continue to make your observations of strength and weakness *as you play*." Thus, this seemingly analytic strategy, the Pie Strategy, has the effect of creating wholeness.

We can now understand Pattern C, a continually changing pattern of weakness, as a continual casting about to fix the weakest quality without a clear picture of how all the pieces fit together. Pattern B reveals an attempt to fix each of two weak qualities without being aware of how the two qualities fit together. To be precise, here is how it might work in Pattern B, where there is a tie for weakest slice between intonation and rhythm: Imagine you just observed that the intonation is the weakest slice. As you make your next observation, your peripheral attention focuses on the intonation. You cannot do it easily, so you slow down on certain notes trying to obey the prime direc-tive (observe *as you play*) while you improve the intonation. You succeed in improving the into-

nation, but the rhythm is now weaker than before. You continue to seesaw back and forth between rhythm and intonation as you observe, resulting in Pattern B. The conclusion you should draw about this particular pattern is that you must learn to play in tune within the framework of a regular beat.

When you first employ the Pie Strategy, it will likely seem strange. In particular, talking out loud when you are alone in your practice room may feel unnatural or bizarre. However, *speaking aloud is of central importance in all steps of the strategy*. In their effort to improve, musicians usually think many diverse thoughts while they are playing. Sometimes they become desperate as they rummage around in their minds for a way to increase their control. When you talk aloud, it clears your mind of other thoughts; it focuses your concentration on your intended purpose. This enhances your observing process and temporarily pushes your other mental tools into the background. (To refresh your memory about mental tools, see Chapter 3, p. 15.) Remember, the purpose of the Pie Strategy (observation) is to highlight the monitoring function, your Observer, in the process of control.

The Berry Strategy

After you've identified the weakest slice, you must identify the particular quality that is lacking and the exact places in the phrase where that quality is poor. For example, if the weakest slice is tone, you must determine *the precise feature of the tone* (i.e., the "berry" in the slice) that is the problem. Here is a list of tonal "berries" (details) that may be missing or of poor quality: clarity, focus, support, core, consistency, depth, character, intensity, timbre, articulation, vocal quality, color, intonation, style, resonance, richness, poignancy, edge, warmth, and brassiness. This list is by no means exhaustive; in an art of sound such as music, tone can and should be differentiated quite elaborately.

If all you observe about the tone is that you do not like the way it sounds, you cannot fix it. If you observe that the tone is not beautiful, you may be able to improve it somewhat. Usually, however, you will make more significant improvement when you can describe the problematic feature as a berry (a detailed aspect of the tone) in the tone slice. For example, if clarity is the offending berry, and you know exactly where in the phrase the problem exists (e.g., in measures 3 and 4), then you will more likely be able to choose or create an appropriate strategy to solve it.

In order to make useful observations, you must be consciously aware of the numerous features (or berries) of each slice that can be manipulated to make music. A list of features (berries) follows. This list is not exhaustive. Please feel free to add to it as you evolve your knowledge and skill as an observer.

Rhythm: evenness, flow, pacing, direction, pulse, articulation, tempo, inflection of rhythmic subdivisions, metric stress, energy, character, playfulness

Tone: clarity, focus, support, core, consistency, depth, character, intensity, timbre, articulation, breathing quality, vocal quality, color, intonation, style, resonance, richness, range, poignancy, edge, warmth, brassiness

Intonation: pitch, tonal support, confidence, melodic and harmonic expression, vibrato, voicing, key organization, mood

Expression (the objective side): structure, phrasing, tension and release, timing, character, pacing, dynamics, expression indications (words/symbols): tempo, rhythmic expression of time signature, articulation, architecture, form, style

Expression (the subjective side): Projection, imagination, color/tone, connection of mood to music, impulsive/free/improvisational, compelling, emotional tension, character, personality, personal conviction, sincerity

The following steps show how you would use the Berry Strategy if you had determined that tone was the weakest slice using the Pie Strategy.

Step 1 Say out loud, "I am going to play from _____ to _____ and observe for the beauty of the tone" (or the excellence, appropriateness, and so on, of the tone).

Step 2 Play the passage.

Step 3 Include two parts to your observation:

a. "I observed that on a scale of 1 to 10 the excellence of the tone was _____." If the number you choose to express the quality is the same throughout, proceed to Step 4. If not, specify where the quality varied. For example: "In measure 3 it was a 7, and in measure 5 it was a 5," etc.

b. Now, focus on places that received the lowest scores and answer the following question: "What did you hear that made you say _____ and not 10?" Your answers to this question will identify the "tonal berries" in the slice that require improvement. For example: "In measure 3 the tone was shrill and in measure 5 the tone was unfocused."

Step 4 Once you have identified the specific weakness in the tone, try a strategy you know to solve the problem, or ask your colleagues or teachers what strategies they use.

When you use the Berry Strategy, it is not necessary to observe repeatedly for the same quality as you did when you used the Pie Strategy. As soon as you know an instrumental strategy that can help you improve the quality that is lacking, try it. Once you hear that you have improved the passage with respect to that quality, use the Berry Strategy again to validate the improvement in the context of a whole phrase or section.

Practicing the Technique of Observation

The Pie Strategy: Identifying the Next Problem to Work On

Step 1 Say out loud: "I am going to play from ___ to ___ and observe for the strongest and weakest slices of the pie."

Step 2 *As you are playing*, observe which is strongest and weakest. Don't practice to improve it; just observe what's there. If you stop, the play-through doesn't count. Start again.

Step 3 Within 10 seconds, say "I observed that the strongest slice was ___, and the weakest slice was ___." If you hesitate, it doesn't count. If you announce the weakest slice first, start again.

Step 4 Write down your observations after each play-through:

Strongest	Weakest

Step 5 Repeat Steps 1 to 4 until you have played the section five times or until three of the weakest slices are the same, whichever comes first.

The Berry Strategy: Determining the Weakest Quality of the Area Needing the Most Work

Step 1 Say out loud: "I am going to play from ___ to ____ and observe for the (beauty/excellence/etc.) of the (tone/rhythm/intonation/expression)." *Choose one from each group.*

Step 2 Play the passage.

Step 3 Say aloud, "I observed that, on a scale of 1 to 10, the (beauty/excellence/etc.) of the (tone/rhythm/intonation/expression) was _____" (fractions are okay). *Or* if the (beauty/excellence/etc.) of the (tone/rhythm/etc.) was uneven through the passage, say "In measure number ___ it was _____ and in measure number ____ it was _____."

Step 4 Ask yourself aloud, "What did I hear that made me say _____ (weakest) and not 10?" An answer might be "In measure 3 the tone was unfocused" (choose the quality that is weakest from the list of berries, p. 34).

Step 5 Try an instrumental strategy you know to solve the problem (see Part Two), or ask your colleagues or teachers what strategies they use.

2 The Technique of Success at Any Cost: Setting an Achievable Goal and Finding a Strategy to Reach It

To Understand

In the lessons and seminars I teach, I often have musicians practice in front of me or the group. They are asked to practice as if they are alone and to do whatever they would do when alone. After 35 years of observing several thousand musicians reveal what is going on behind the closed doors of their practice chamber, I have found one particularly counterproductive common denominator. They try to do more than is possible in the available time and with the available "space" in their mind. There is little sense of fulfillment from day to day. Each musician seems to be responding to unconscious expectations governed by personal and emotional factors rather than objective and conscious ones. The result is a sense of urgency and anxiety and a self-image of inadequacy based on an uneasy awareness that their unconscious expectations are rarely fulfilled. No wonder, then, that negative feelings surface at the moment of concert performance, often causing debilitating anxiety and disappointment.

Comfort in Practicing: The Light of Informed Consciousness

Studies of skill development show that concentration and growth will be at a maximum if you simply do what you can do from day to day without concern for when you will achieve the final result. If you hurry to achieve a goal, or if your goal includes more than you can handle, your capacity to achieve that goal will be diminished in proportion to your greed.*

During the second half of the twentieth century, a vast body of information was collected and published revealing how people acquire skill. This knowledge has already been extensively integrated into the teaching of athletic skills.† Although it is particularly applicable to training musicians to practice effectively, it is only gradually seeping into music pedagogy. At this time, there is no cohesive practice pedagogy. Musicians continue to suffer from a lack of informed consciousness to guide their practicing. The Technique of Success at Any Cost offers the musician a conscious and efficient way to form achievable goals, maximize concentration, and adjust to realistic expectations.

Because the first two myths of practicing are intimately related to controlling expectations, you might want to refresh your memory about them

---

*Sternberg and Kolligian, *Competence Considered.*
† See, for example, Loehr, *The New Toughness Training for Sports.*

before going on to study the Technique of Success at Any Cost (see Chapter 3). This technique will help you adjust your expectations and deal effectively with frustration and concentration. It will enable you to use your best concentration to achieve new levels of sensitivity and technical control on a daily basis.

Your Concentration Is Your Best Friend, Even When It Lets You Down

Concentration is an energy that shuts itself off when the goal is too hard (frustrating) *and* when it is too easy (boring). When the purpose of employing your concentration is to reach an achievable goal (not too hard and not too easy), it offers itself easily, until normal physical fatigue sets in.

Unfortunately, as we all know too well, innumerable ordinary life circumstances can inhibit our concentration. We may be too tired to concentrate. Or we may be distracted by concerns of varying levels of importance: anxiety about having enough money, being unprepared for our performance tomorrow, being rejected by a friend or lover, having too little time to practice, or hunger. These are just a few of life's distractions, but there are strategies to control these distractions.* Here, I will address how to control concentration when the life environment is distraction-free and time is available to practice.

Consider this practice scenario: A musician is practicing to perfect the intonation (rhythm, phrasing, etc.) in the third octave of an A♭ major scale. After 4 consecutive days of trying, he observes that the scale is no more in tune than it was 4 days before. As he tries once again to perfect the intonation, he finds that his mind is wandering. He cannot maintain his concentration, and he is beginning to feel impatient and frustrated. A little voice inside gives advice: "You must keep working on the intonation each day. Eventually your work will pay off. It is a difficult problem, but ultimately you will succeed." This is the time-honored method. "Do not give up! Keep trying!"

There *are* instances where this philosophy can be particularly effective. For example, imagine that you're digging a garden that is to cover an area of 2500 square feet. The soil is packed with rocks and clay. You wake up filled with energy and go out anticipating the great joy of working up a sweat. As you are a perfectionist, you have set yourself the goal of turning over the earth to a depth of 1 foot and removing every rock larger than a diameter of one-quarter of an inch. Three hours later you look around at your work. You have succeeded brilliantly but you have only completed a 5-by-10-foot plot, amounting to 50 square feet. You feel frustrated and impatient. Your inner voice gives advice: "If you keep working each day your work will pay off. Do not give up. Keep trying." As you sit down to rest you calculate that if you work 3 hours each day, you will complete the job in 50 days. You feel justifiably satisfied that if you follow the advice of your inner voice, you will succeed.

But what about the frustrated and impatient practicer we left two paragraphs back? Unlike the gardener, he may "dig up" a perfect note on one day only to find that it is no longer there the next day, or the next minute, for that matter. He cannot estimate when he will achieve his goal. It is likely that even if he practices the A♭ major scale for a whole year, he may never be able to perform his scale perfectly in tune, every time he plays it.†

If that is true, then his concentration is acting like a true friend when it deserts him. Sensing the impossibility of the task, his concentration gives up, thereby sending the message: "What you are trying to do is impossible. *Stop playing, now!* Set a more reasonable goal. This is not paying off."

At these moments we often demand of ourselves that we concentrate harder. Our coaches demand it in our lessons, so it is not strange that we demand it of ourselves during practice. Have you ever watched a person trying to concentrate harder (Figure 5-4)? People seem to have a universal tendency to tighten inappropriate muscles

---

* Thoughts that distract us while we practice usually repeat obsessively throughout our practice. They demand immediate attention and they come with a fear that we will forget them or have no time to deal with them. To control distracting thoughts that intrude while you practice, try this: Keep a notepad on your music stand. Whenever a distracting thought occurs, note it on the pad, along with when you plan to deal with it. Usually this procedure reduces the anxiety and the obsessive need for its repetition, and the thought goes away.

† Musicians who play instruments that require control of intonation (unlike the piano) work for hours and years to control their intonation precisely. It is of some interest to note that "research on the intervals played or sung by skilled musicians shows substantial variability in the intonation from performance to performance" (Ward, "Musical Perception").

Figure 5-4 *Musicians trying to concentrate harder during practice.*

when they are trying to achieve a goal without success. The tension often starts in the eyes. Then the neck stiffens in an effort to help the eyes steady their gaze. Before long the tension level in the entire body is considerably elevated, while the concentration continues to slip away because it is incapable of working harder. Concentration either works or does not work. It intensifies only if the goal requires more of it. Should you demand more than its true capacity, it will slip away, encouraging you to find a different approach to your practice.

To improve your concentration, change your goal to one you can achieve. In addition, you will find that the Rule of Impatience (Chapter 6) is a powerful guide to maintaining your concentration. If the musician practicing the A♭ major scale knew a different strategy (such as playing only the tonic and the dominant in tune and ignoring the intonation of the other notes), then his concentration might have returned in full bloom. The command "Concentrate harder!" cannot achieve the desired effect. To summarize, *concentration flourishes in the worlds of the possible and the probable*. It shuns the impossible like the plague.

Using the Technique of Success at Any Cost to Improve Concentration and Control Expectations

The purpose of the Technique of Success at Any Cost is twofold: (1) ***to set an achievable goal*** and (2) ***to know or create a strategy to achieve that goal.*** An achievable goal is not too hard (frustrat-

ing), not too easy (boring), and attainable without physical strain within a short time. Chapter 3 and Chapters 8 to 14 contain strategies you can use to improve. The Table of Contents lists most of the strategies described in the book.

Step 1 Pick a passage to improve.

Step 2 Using the Technique of Observation, decide which aspect of your playing to address (the slice) and what specifically you mean to fix (the berry).

Step 3 Choose a strategy that enables you to make an improvement in a short time *without physical strain*. As part of your effort to establish an achievable goal without strain, simplify the problem, or reduce the demand. The Simplification Strategy (Chapter 9) offers many ways to do this. Read it now to appreciate the many ways in which you can simplify a problem to create a more effective practice regimen.

> *Keep in mind that more often than not, the Simplification Strategy is only part of a multi-strategy approach to solving a problem. Often you must implement several related strategies simultaneously to improve a passage. This will become clearer when you read Chapter 9. Whatever strategies you choose, apply them in the context of the Technique of Success at Any Cost.*

Special Instructions

a. Use the Rule of Selective Inattention (Chapter 6) to avoid becoming distracted by qualities that are not your primary focus.

b. Protect yourself from frustration when necessary by using the Rule of Impatience (Chapter 6).

Step 4 If you cannot improve a passage as described above, pay the ultimate price: Change your expectations entirely. Go on to another passage now; try again later; try again tomorrow; seek more information from a friend or colleague; or wait until your lesson for advice.

Step 5 When you achieve your goal the first time, acknowledge your success by saying **out loud to yourself, "Good job!"**

When I teach this technique, I find that many practicers find it difficult to congratulate themselves in this simple, open way because they have conditioned themselves to believe that the *only* good job is the complete and perfect one. This underlying attitude of discontent has the effect of a slow poison. It diminishes concentration and reduces endurance. When these same people offer themselves the support of deserved self-approbation, their concentration is enhanced and the process of work becomes more pleasurable and meaningful. I offer the following realistic and comforting advice as an antidote to the slow poison of perfectionist desires:

Better is perfect, and PERFECT is irrelevant!

It should be apparent that to succeed in setting an achievable goal you must pay the price of lowering your expectations, hence, the Technique of Success *at Any Cost*. The "price" you pay for lowering your expectations is delaying your need for gratification to achieve the final product. It is only costly because musicians are often bound by unrealistic expectations; they have become addicted to the tension of demanding more than is possible day after day.

Rather than strain to perfect a phrase in one session, divide your work on the phrase into sub-steps. Simplify your goals so that each sub-step can, in one session, be controlled to a higher-quality level *without strain*. At first, you will feel that it will take you forever to perfect the whole phrase, but in fact, it is the fastest way.

It is amazing how often practicers try and fail to achieve the same impossible goals daily, thus building strain and inconsistency into their final product. If, instead, they master each sub-step on the way to mastering the whole, the result can only be successful, as there is barely a memory trace of failure in the process of work. Like it or not, your performances will reflect, at best, only the *average* of all your practice efforts.

In other words, to condition your system to produce performance consistency, *you must succeed to succeed.* The true source of stage fright is the unacknowledged memory of inconsistency and feelings of inadequacy in the practice room. *By using the Technique of Success at Any Cost, you can prevent performance anxiety.*

Practicing the Technique of Success at Any Cost

Step 1 Pick a passage to improve.

Step 2 Using the Technique of Observation, decide which quality is lacking (i.e., the weakest slice and the chosen berry). Choose only one quality at a time.

Step 3 Choose a strategy that enables you to make an improvement in a short time, without physical strain. Begin with the Simplification Strategy (Chapter 9) as part of a multiple-strategy approach.

Special Instructions

a. Use the Rule of Selective Inattention (Chapter 6) to avoid becoming distracted by qualities that are not your primary focus.

b. Protect yourself from frustration when necessary by using the Rule of Impatience (Chapter 6).

Step 4 If you can't make an improvement easily, change your expectations. Try again later or tomorrow; ask for advice from a teacher or colleague.

Step 5 When you achieve your goal the first time, say "Good job!" *out loud* to yourself.

Keep in mind that an improvement, though not perfection, is perfet enough because it is possible: *"Better is perfect and PERFECT is irrelevant!"*

3 The Technique of Intimacy: Stabilizing the New Success

To Understand

The human system does not naturally behave with the regularity and reliability of a machine. In spite of this, as performing musicians, we continue to demand a machine-like precision of ourselves. In the best live public performances it appears to be close to possible, and audio and video recordings attest to an even greater technical perfection than we hear in live performances.* There are two ways to achieve this extraordinary state of performance control. One is to be a prodigy who finds the way with minimal help. The other is to be one of the-rest-of-us, needing a detailed functional understanding of the limitations of human nature to succeed.

A key to this understanding is the following concept: *Your body is a dog*. Like the dog, your body is capable of being conditioned to perform a sequence of actions reflexively, without conscious direction. When a dog first learns a new trick, such as giving its paw on command, it can easily forget the trick by tomorrow unless it does the trick over and over correctly today, and tomorrow—*and* tomorrow. Like the dog, *your* body will likely forget tomorrow the trick (improvement) it learned today unless you repeat the trick over and over correctly today, and tomorrow—and tomorrow. Your body's confidence grows proportionally as you are rewarded by your success.

Technique Is Memory

It hit me like a bolt of lightning when I first realized that technique is memory. In other words, at each moment in my practice I am either trying to refine my skill to a new level or trying to remember the refinement until the refinement seems to remember itself. That moment when control is automatic, when I can "do the trick" without conscious direction, is *the goal* sine qua non of practice. We want to memorize the skill so that it is reflexive.

Fortunately, in the last quarter of the twentieth century, memory has been investigated extensively by psychology and neuroscience.† Two results of this research are of great significance for learning to practice a musical instrument: (1) There is a limit to how much the human mind can remember at any particular moment‡ and (2) short-term and long-term memory are controlled by two different parts of the brain.†† One of the values of using the Technique of Success at Any Cost is that it helps you to set a realistic limit to your expectations of remembering today's improvements tomorrow. The Technique of Intimacy gives you a reliable procedure to achieve consistent, reflexive memory of refinements you make from day to day, which then leads inevitably to secure control during performance.

To understand how and why the Technique of Intimacy works, you need to understand the difference between short-term and long-term memory. *Short-term memory* refers to the ephemeral nature of memory during the first 24 hours after you have tried to commit something to memory. Memory experiments have shown that at the end of 24 hours we should expect to forget 50% or more of what we tried to remember. On the other hand, if you continue to repeat the same memory effort each day for 4 or 5 days, the long-term memory part of the brain gradually begins to take over. In 4 or 5 days, *long-term memory is set* and you experience an internal sensation of ease, as if the

---

* These audio and video recordings create an illusion of human perfection through editing of the real performances. It is an illusion because the recordings are electronically altered versions of actual performances. Tiny imperfections can be, and are, deleted and improved versions are put in their place. Therefore, what the listener hears rarely, if ever, occurs in one take in a live performance. But we are seduced by the recording to try to duplicate it, nevertheless.

† Damasio, *The Feeling of What Happens*, short-term memory, pp. 112–117.

‡ Johnson, *In the Palaces of Memory*, pp. 22–23 and 43–44 especially. Goldberg, *Executive Brain*, pp. 72–77.

†† Strogatz, *Sync*, pp. 280–281.

memory had always been there. This is a feeling state I characterize as "useful boredom." Your need to focus your concentration to achieve the result diminishes, and you find that, though your mind may begin to wander, your skill continues to be in your control.

To understand the influence of memory on skill development better, consider this: In a typical practice session, musicians try to refine many passages to bring them closer to a performance standard. Imagine practicing to improve the rhythmic accuracy of a phrase. You must repeat parts of the phrase many times to define the desired timing of a number of notes. It is a painstaking process. We will refer to each repetition the musician makes to refine intonation as one of the different Xs in the following description: X̊ represents the starting point of work on the intonation; X́ represents some improvement and X̀ further improvement. A ✔ represents a successful, improved play-through.

$$ \overset{o}{X} \quad \overset{\prime}{X} \quad \overset{o}{X} \quad \overset{\prime}{X} \quad \overset{\prime}{X} \quad \overset{\prime}{X} \quad \overset{\prime}{X} \quad \overset{\prime}{X} \quad X \quad \checkmark $$

In this instance, the practicer succeeds on the tenth try. It is a moment when he feels that the problem is solved. He worked hard, he got the job done, and now he feels fulfilled. Most practicers at this point go on to refine another phrase or try to improve another quality that is lacking. Some will try to repeat the success one or two times, right away. If it works, fine. If it does not work, they are usually too frustrated to start over again. This pattern of work leads to the frequent complaint "I often feel that I have to start over again each day." But is there any rational basis for the belief that tomorrow the success achieved on the tenth try will be available immediately? On the contrary, an average of 1 success in 10 tries would, at best, give us a 10% chance of producing that success tomorrow. If we take into consideration the fickle nature of short-term memory, we should expect only a 5% chance of success. On further reflection it is obvious that, in the example above, the overwhelming experience in our memory is of incorrectness, not of correctness. Therefore, we should not expect to play the passage better tomorrow than we did today.

Using the Technique of Intimacy to Develop Consistent Control of an Improvement

At the first moment of success, ✔, your short-term memory is most in your control. It is at this moment, before your memory of the success fades, that you have a chance to increase the proportion of successes to failures. If at this moment you can change your percentage of success from 10% to 50% or more, then your last memories from today will favor your success tomorrow.

I call this process the Technique of Intimacy because it refers to experiences we all have had throughout our lives. If you go out on a date and you have a good time, you naturally feel like going out again with the same person. Each time you go out you become more intimate, more *familiar* with that person. If you see each other often, the mental image of that person can be startlingly real even when he or she is not present. Your memory is enhanced by repeating the experience. Isn't that what you want when you practice, to become so familiar with your success that it is impossible to forget it? Therefore, immediately after your first success and the glow of satisfaction that accompanies it, use the Technique of Intimacy. Remember that at the end of the Technique of Success at Any Cost you acknowledged your success by saying, "Good job!" *out loud*. **Immediately after this acknowledgment,** begin Step 1 of the Technique of Intimacy:

Step 1 Try to *repeat your success 5 times in no more than 10 tries.*

Step 2 Record the number of tries it takes you to repeat your success, for example, 5/9 (5 successes in 9 tries), on the Success and Intimacy Collection Sheet (Figure 5-5). In addition, write the goal and approximately how long it took you to achieve your first success. Using this information, you will be able to measure your progress tomorrow. If you succeed, you can skip Step 3 and go on to Step 4.

If, on the other hand, you are at 1/7, you should not continue because you have no chance of achieving 5 successes within 10 tries. If that happens, stop, and proceed to Step 3.

Success and Intimacy Collection Sheet

Piece, Movement, Etude _____

Quality and Goals	Day 1	Day 2	Day 3	Day 4	Day 5	Ideas

Figure 5-5 *The complete chart for copying is in the Appendix.*

Step 3 If you are unable to achieve 5 successes in no more than 10 tries, stop trying. Use the Technique of Success at Any Cost to change your goal. Simplify your goal until you succeed at Steps 1 and 2 *or* return to the Technique of Success at Any Cost tomorrow.

Step 4 If you have achieved 5 successes in no more than 10 tries, go on to work on the next passage. Do not pay any more attention to this passage today. *Avoid the temptation of adding more detail to the passage you now seem to know so well.* It is only temporarily stable. If you have already spent 5 minutes or more to refine the phrase, adding more detail will overload your memory and you will be disappointed in your control tomorrow.

Step 5 Tomorrow, start by trying to play the same passage with the same goal. If it is not immediately in your control at the same level, practice to return to the control of yesterday. *Do not increase the difficulty of the goal.* The first sign of your progress is that you will find that it takes less time today to achieve your first success than it took yesterday. Now, repeat Steps 1, 2, and 4. You can expect that your ratio of successes to failures will be better than yesterday. You now have two concrete measures of progress toward consistency: (1) less time to reach your first success and (2) fewer repetitions to achieve five successes.

Step 6 *Repeat the same procedure for 4 days.* By the fourth day you will have achieved either 5/5 or 5/6. If you achieved 5/5, you are ready to further improve the quality or increase the tempo. If you achieved 5/6, it means that some aspect of the skill needed to achieve the result is a little unstable. Either try to figure out what that instability is *or* try to further improve the quality *or* increase the tempo anyway, aware that there is some instability in the base on which you are building.

Pitfalls and Benefits

Though the Technique of Intimacy is simple to understand, it is difficult to fulfill. As you proceed from Step 1 to Step 6, it is important to avoid some pitfalls in order to receive maximum benefit from the technique. They are described in detail below as a set of rules.

Rules

Rule 1 *Each time you try to repeat your success, play through to the end without stopping in spite of whatever flaws or errors you hear.* Each time you repeat the phrase, if you find you are dissatisfied with what you hear, *do not stop to try to improve it.* It is important to separate the part of the practice process in which you search to refine the product (the Technique of Success at Any Cost) from the part where you stabilize your success (the Technique of Intimacy). When we search to establish refinement, we allow ourselves endless tries to succeed, but when we play through, we always expect a first-try success, as in a performance. The Technique of Intimacy is the beginning of the practice to perform the product consistently with confidence on your first try.

Rule 2 *If you achieve 5 successes in 5 tries on the first day, your goal is too easy.* Improve the passage further. If you achieve 5/5 on the second day, your work is done. Improve the passage further unless it is already excellent.

Rule 3 *If after 4 or 5 days, you do not achieve at least 5/6, STOP.* You need more information or additional help to master this control. It is at this point in the practice process that a meaningful student-teacher dialogue can occur. It would improve the efficiency of a 1-hour lesson considerably if each student were independent enough to go this far before the lesson.

Rule 4 *To develop consistent control, you must practice on consecutive days.* Skipping a day increases the possibility of forgetting. Remember: When you have the feeling that your control is automatic, your control is stored in long-term memory. Keep in mind also that, *until your control has become part of long-term memory,* your confidence and consistency of control will not be at an optimum level if you leave daily gaps of a day or more in your practice schedule.

Notice that the Technique of Intimacy benefits both the overly obsessive musician and the overly optimistic musician. Overly obsessive musicians who would repeat their success too many times are protected from wasting time. Unjustifiably optimistic musicians, who would repeat it only one or two times, if at all, are protected from disappointment tomorrow.

The Technique of Intimacy also yields a still more subtle benefit. There is an important difference between setting a goal to achieve 5 successes in 5 tries and setting a goal to achieve 5 successes in no more than 10 tries over a period of 4 or 5 days. In the latter instance, though you may hope that 5/5 will result in the near future, you are man-

aging your daily effort to increase your percentage of success. This prevents you from becoming too anxious about when you will achieve 5/5. Your concern with achieving 5/5 is more a curiosity about whether it will happen than urgency that it does happen. When 5/5 occurs, it happens in the same inevitable way that you eventually reach the supermarket when you leave your house, as long as you keep walking toward it.

On the other hand, the urgency and anxiety you experience when your primary intention is to achieve 5/5 is significantly higher. Inevitably, our state of mind during practice becomes part of the action we are conditioning. Therefore, using the Technique of Intimacy as a guide to consistency prevents building anxiety into our performance conditioning and inadvertently builds ease and confidence instead.

Practicing the Technique of Intimacy

Step 1 At the end of the Technique of Success at Any Cost, you said, "Good job!" Immediately after you say it, try to repeat your success 5 times in no more than 10 tries.

Step 2 Record the number of tries it takes you to repeat your success (e.g., 5/9) on the Success and Intimacy Collection Sheet (see Figure 5-5). Also record the goal and approximately how long it took you to achieve your first success. If you succeed you can skip Step 3 and go on to Step 4.

Step 3 If you don't achieve 5 successes in 10 tries, STOP. Use the technique of Success at Any Cost to change your goal, *or* start again tomorrow. Then repeat Steps 1 and 2 above.

Step 4 Work on another passage. Don't pay any more attention to the passage you just completed today.

Step 5 Tomorrow repeat Steps 1 and 2. You will have progressed if it takes less time to achieve your first success and if your percentage of success is improved (e.g., 5/8).

Step 6 Repeat the same procedure for 4 consecutive days. By the fourth day you will have achieved 5/5 or 5/6. Now you are ready to improve the passage further—to increase speed, quality, or some other factor.

Rules

Rule 1 Each time you try to repeat your success, play through without stopping to the end of the phrase, ignoring all errors.

Rule 2 If you achieve 5 successes in 5 tries the first day, your goal is too easy. Improve the passage further. If you achieve 5/5 the second day, your work is done. Improve the passage further, unless it is already excellent.

Rule 3 If after 4 or 5 days you do not achieve at least 5/6, STOP and reset your goal(s).

Rule 4 To develop consistent control, you must practice *on consecutive days*.

4 The Technique of the First Try: Testing Performance Control

To Understand

It is both mysterious and tragic that after practicing several hundred hours for a performance, a musician can be disappointed with the result. I would like to clear up the mystery and describe a simple, practical solution to this problem that anyone can try. Let us reexamine the problem, considering what the performer is afraid of and the source of those fears.

"What are you nervous about?" I have asked this question of hundreds of people. The answers are always the same: "I'm afraid I'll mess up. I won't play as well as I know I can." "It's difficult to concentrate well when an audience is present." "What if they don't like the way I play?"

Are these fears only fantasy, or are they justified? To answer this question, I reexamined the conditions of performance to describe the variables for which the artist must prepare. I also observed many musicians practicing to find out how they actually prepared for their performances. I observed that performers' fears are usually justified because their preparation is not precisely organized to deal with the realities of the performance situation.

What are the important differences between performing conditions and practicing conditions? Most performers point to the distracting presence of the audience and the need for the approval of the audience as the primary differences. Two other performance realities are rarely mentioned. First, in our culture, you perform at a prearranged time whether or not you feel perfectly ready to do so, feel unwell, feel uncomfortable because you ate too much, or don't feel like performing at that moment. Second, you get one try. You start once, you continue "come hell or high water," and it's over. It was partly for this reason that Glenn Gould left the concert stage. He considered a live audience a great liability. He resented the "one-timeness" of live performance. If he was not pleased with how his performance was going, he wanted to be able to stop, turn to the audience, and say, "Take two."

I have left many practicers alone to be videotaped by an unmanned camera. Later I reviewed the tapes to observe how they prepared for their performance. I discovered that none of them organized their practicing to accommodate the above-mentioned performance realities (i.e., that you must produce a satisfying performance on the first try, at a prearranged moment, on a prearranged day).

In a typical practice session, practicers would "warm up" to prepare for their play-throughs, often polishing the work to be performed for 5 to 30 minutes or more. They would begin with a play-through of moderate success, polish it again for a while, and then, when they felt well primed, play it through with a feeling of fulfillment and satisfaction. Sometimes, they would start to play it through but stop after a few phrases, discontent with the result. Then they would begin again, eventually getting into the rhythm of it and continuing to the end. Afterward, in discussion about the performance preparation, each practicer remembered his best play-through of the day or week as representative of his performance capability. In other words, the best play-through became the performance expectation. No specific effort was made to test his ability to produce the best play-through constrained by the basic performance conditions: on the first try, at a prearranged moment, on a prearranged day.

To help the practicer develop a realistic expectation of performance success, I created a First-Try Chart and a technique for its use (Figure 5-6).

First-Try Chart

Piece or Movement _____					
AS PERFORMER			**AS AUDIENCE**		
Day	% of Success + Problems	Accept? Y/N	Day	% of Success + Problems	Accept? Y/N

Figure 5-6 *The complete chart for copying is in the Appendix.*

Using the First-Try Technique to Practice Performing with Consistent Control

Step 1 When you feel that the work you are preparing to perform is ready, test its readiness at least 6 days in a row (i.e., 6 "practice performances"). The day before each practice performance, decide at what time tomorrow you will perform it.

Step 2 Each day, set up your tape recorder in advance so that it is ready to record your performance. Label a tape and insert it. You should only have to push "power on" and "record" to start recording.

Step 3 If dressing in concert clothes makes you feel different about yourself when you play, you should be dressed in your concert clothes for your first tries.

Step 4 Set an alarm to go off 3 minutes before your practice performance time. Before the alarm rings, practice anything EXCEPT the work you will perform. Warm up in any way you want and as long as you want, but *do not play or practice the work you will perform.*

Step 5 When the alarm rings, turn on your tape recorder, press "record," and walk out of the practice room into the "wings" (a corner of the room will do). Begin to get in the mood for your prac-tice performance by imagining the sound and feel of the piece you will play. Then, walk out, bow, and perform. Once you start, *you may not stop until the performance is over.* Second tries are not allowed. If you have a memory slip, do whatever you would do in a real performance.

Step 6 When your performance is over, express your general impression of the degree of success as a percentage on your First-Try Chart (see Figure 5-7 for an example). In addition, make detailed notes on your chart of sections and spots that your practice performance indicated as needing more work. Indicate whether you would consider this performance successful if it were your actual performance. You may answer only yes or no.

Step 7 Now, listen to the tape recording of your first-try performance. Record your observations on the First-Try Chart. Compare your impressions "as performer" with those made "as audience."

Part of the aim of comparing your impression as a performer with your impression as an audience is to learn to hear as a performer the way you hear as an audience. Practicing to improve the problems you noticed on the First-Try Chart each day and to deal with the disparity between your impressions as a performer and as an audience will give you valuable insight to improve your control as a performer.

Step 8 When you have done 6 practice performances on 6 consecutive days, you are ready to evaluate your expectations for success in an actual performance. If your last four first tries would have been acceptable to you as actual performances, it is realistic to expect a performance in the range of your last four first tries. If one or more of your last four first tries would not have been acceptable as a performance, the probability of a performance that will please you is considerably diminished. It is not reasonable to present a performance in public that does not make you proud when you are alone.

In my experience, most players who have succeeded in achieving four acceptable first tries in a row find that they can achieve that level in performance, that their pleasure while performing is enhanced, and that their anxiety is considerably diminished. Incidentally, even players who do not achieve four acceptable first tries find that they perform as well as they did in their practice room, or better. I have concluded that using the First-Try technique in the practice room establishes realistic expectations for the performer. As a consequence, the actual performance is a confirmation of what the performer can do instead of a set of surprising disappointments.

Practicing the First-Try Technique

Step 1 When you feel that the piece you are preparing to perform is ready, test its readiness at least 6 days in a row. The day before each practice performance, decide at what time on the next day you will perform it.

Step 2 The day of your trial performance, set up your recording device so that you only have to push "on" and "record" to start recording.

Step 3 Dress in your concert clothes if it makes you feel different.

Step 4 Each day, set an alarm to go off 3 minutes before your performance time. Before the alarm rings, practice anything EXCEPT the work you will perform. Warm up in any way you want and as long as you want, but do not play or practice the work you will perform.

Step 5 When the alarm rings, turn on your recorder, press "record," and walk "back stage." Get in the mood by imagining the sound and feel of the piece. Then, walk out, bow, and perform. You may not stop until the performance is over. Do everything as you would in a real performance.

First-Try Chart

Piece or Movement _____

	AS PERFORMER			AS AUDIENCE	
Day	% of Success + Problems	Accept? Y/N	Day	% of Success + Problems	Accept? Y/N
1/3	*80%* *M. 32-38, intonation, sharp* *M. 40-44, tone, scratchy* *M. 50, L/R coordination*	*N*	1/3	*85%* *M. 32-38, intonation, sharp* *M. 50, L/R coordination* *M. 54-60, tone, thin*	*N*
1/4	*85%*	*N*	1/4	*88%*	*Y*

Figure 5-7

Step 6 In the left column, "As Performer," on your First-Try Chart, express your general impression of the degree of success of your performance as a percentage of 100. Also indicate (Y or N) whether or not this performance would be acceptable if it were the real one. (Figure 5-7 shows a First-Try Chart filled in correctly.) Make detailed notes as to what needs work.

Step 7 Listen to your recording and fill in your impressions as in Step 6 in the right column, "As Audience." Compare your impressions as a performer with those made as an audience. Use this information in your continuing practice each day.

Step 8 Repeat this process once each day for 5 more consecutive days. You can realistically expect to achieve an average of your last 4 first tries in your actual performance.

Impediments to Success with First Tries

• It may be that on the day of performance your level of excitement rises so high that your system is in an essentially different state than in your practice room. For musicians with this experience, meditating, deep muscle relaxation, and imaging can be of great help. For specific help along these lines, read David Sternbach's articles, "Overcoming Playing Anxiety," *International Musician*, March 1988 and July 1989. Another useful guide is James Loehr's book, *New Toughness Training in Sports*. You can also try Daniel Goleman's excellent tape, *The Relaxed Body*. In addition, ask your physician if he would advise trying some of the beta-blocker drugs on the market, such as propranolol (Inderal). To learn more, read R.J. Lederman, "Medical Treatment of Performance Anxiety: A Statement in Favor," *Medical Problems of Performing Artists*, 1999, 14(3):117-121.

• If none of these solutions helps you, you may wish to explore psychotherapeutic approaches to the problem. You might begin by reading two articles: Eric A. Plaut, "Psychotherapy of Performance Anxiety," *Medical Problems of Performing Artists*, 1988, 3:113–118, and Kyle D. Pruett, "Young Narcissus at the Music Stand: Developmental Perspectives from Embarrassment to Exhibitionism," *Medical Problems of Performing Artists*, 1988, 2:69–75.

• What if after reaching an acceptable first-try performance level in an actual performance, you are not satisfied? Investigate the accuracy of your perception. Save your recordings of first tries in the practice studio and compare them to recordings of actual performances. If you do not find the answer, listen with a teacher, coach, or another musician. You need more information.

• What if you perform, think it's awful, and upon hearing a recording of your performance, you're surprised to find that its quality IS acceptable? Just keep performing. Experience solves this problem.

Additional Thoughts on the Basic Work Process

Do not underestimate the complexity of consciously embracing the techniques of the Basic Work Process and integrating them into your practice: It will be a huge change. There are several experiences you should anticipate when you use the techniques in an actual practice session.

Time and the Basic Work Process

Whenever you add meaningful managerial procedures to your practice, your work will benefit. It is best, however, to add the techniques of the Basic Work Process to your practice when you are ***not under pressure to perform.***

You need time to rehearse each technique as an exercise until it becomes part of your reflexive thought and behavior. Then you need time to experience using the techniques sequentially with ease. And although you may find great pleasure in controlling your expectations consciously, managing your practice more intelligently, and replacing your "Interior Gremlin" (that nagging, negative inner voice) with a pleasurable rhythm of day-to-day progress, you will have to struggle to alter your habits. The more time you can make available for this transformation, the more successful you will be. Six months is realistic. If you do not have the luxury of that amount of time, explore each technique for a week or a month at a time. If you are thorough in your approach for at least one week at a time, you will notice the results pay off gradually over time.

One way to incorporate some study of the Basic Work Process on a regular basis, whether or not you are preparing for a performance, is to reserve a minimum of 30 minutes during each practice to work on the four techniques unconstrained by time. In other words, during the time you set aside for this purpose, do not set goals that create expectations that you achieve specific performance results in set amounts of time. Just exercise the techniques to find out more about how they work and what you can expect of them. Your progress will be slow but steady if you can discipline yourself in this way.

The Formality of Your New Practice Space

The practice space of most musicians is relatively informal. When you are hungry, you stop to snack. When you plan to play through a piece and you are discontent with the result before you reach the end, you start again. As you have seen, the techniques of the Basic Work Process are quite formal. Here are a few thoughts about how to explore and integrate the new formality into your work:

- Practice each of the four techniques as a daily etude for a week or two. Try them out many times in different kinds of compositions. Start by spending 10 to 20 minutes during each practice using each technique. As you experience each technique from day to day, you will develop a heightened awareness of its value. It would be unreasonable to expect yourself to integrate the techniques into a coherently managed package until each step is quite familiar.

- The techniques of the Basic Work Process are used for refinement; *do not use them for starting work on a new piece or etude.* Instead, begin your work on new repertoire as described in Chapter 1, p. 10. After 2 weeks or more, however, the novelty of new repertoire begins to wear off and patterns of success and failure begin to emerge. It is at this moment, when you notice that not much improvement occurs from day to day, that the use of these techniques will pay off significantly. Or, when you find that you are bored, unduly frustrated, or have "hit a wall" in the way of meaningful progress, try the techniques and guide your work by their formal rules.

- As you become familiar with these new habits of mind on a daily basis, you will find your mind following their path even when you do not think meticulously about them.

- At the risk of being redundant, I feel compelled to remind you that in a performance art, understanding is doing. It is much easier to "understand" ideas than to direct your actions by them. It is only after you have exercised the techniques in your practice over a period of 4 to 6 months that you can say you truly ***understand*** them because you are expert at ***doing*** them.

A Fringe Benefit of the Pie Strategy

There is a hidden benefit to using the Pie Strategy (p. 30). When using the Pie Strategy, the musician is compelled to attend to the musical whole as a point of reference in order to determine the relative strength and weakness of each slice of the pie. As a result, he will often unconsciously make integrating adjustments of the slices so they make sense as a whole. In other words, this seemingly analytic technique has the paradoxical effect of binding the pieces holistically together. Some musicians have found this experience so profound that they just repeat the Pie Strategy on parts of the music, and the miracle of integration occurs all by itself.

Live in the Achievable Present, not the Unattainable Future

When musicians use the Basic Work Process in a formal way, they often think, "At this rate, I'll never finish this piece." That is what it feels like at first to practice in the reality of the present instead of the unattainable future.

Return for a moment to the picture of the donkey continually striving for the unreachable carrot (p. 16) to be reminded of the folly of that attitude. If you trust yourself to be guided consciously by the techniques to achieve small steps each day, you will be able to look back after a few weeks and notice significant progress. It is quite like watching a flower evolve from a bud into full bloom. The subjective sensation is that "A watched flower never blooms" (a paraphrasing of "A watched pot never boils"). But if you return to the bud after a few days, the flower will have bloomed, fulfilling your expectations.

In the simplest terms, you must learn to practice the way you climb a mountain. Your long-term goal is to reach the top of the mountain. Each step you take gets you closer to the top. If as you take each step you torture yourself with thoughts of how many more steps you must take to get to the top, the journey will seem endless. If, instead, you enjoy the pleasure of each step without continually thinking of how far away the top is, you will get there and you will have enjoyed the hike as well. Though it is easy to say and hard to do, *it can be done.*

CHAPTER 6

Patience and Attention:
Two Practice Traps

We are all taught that "patience is a virtue," and that we should "pay attention," but there are pragmatic limits to these virtues. The lucky musician realizes this and adjusts her practice habits accordingly. Most musicians, however, feel compelled to persist even when they are not achieving the results they want. This chapter focuses on avoiding the potential traps of patience and attention.

Impatience as Practice Power

One of the big mistakes musicians make when they practice is that they often try to solve problems by "playing through" them. Now why would a person do that? It is likely that continual repetition will reinforce a problem, not lead to a solution. The person who keeps playing through a problem without stopping to reflect is expressing either too much patience—unrealistically waiting for a revelation—or too much impatience—being too driven to stop and confront her frustration intelligently. We greatly value patience, but as with all valued human behaviors, there is a boundary beyond which it can be counterproductive. To protect yourself from excessive patience, follow the Rule of Impatience: ***When patience is no longer productive, impatience is the greater good.***

The Rule of Impatience

When, in your effort to improve, you repeat a detail, a phrase, or a section of a piece *three times* *in a row* without success, ***stop playing! Give up!*** Stop pursuing your goal in the particular manner you have been employing and take time to reflect on other options. You could:

- Try a different strategy if you know one.

- Try to invent a new strategy.

- Practice something else and plan to return to the problem later in the same practice.

- Practice something else and wait until tomorrow to return to this part.

- Wait until your lesson for new advice.

- Go for a walk and come back refreshed to practice further.

- Call friends or colleagues and ask them about their strategies for dealing with the same type of problem.

- Read some books about strategies to improve this type of problem.

- Read books about anything but music, hoping for inspiration to come to you "out of left field " (heuristic and lateral thinking*).

In fact, effective practice should contain many pauses for reflection. I would go so far as to say that reflection is *central* to effective music practice. On average, insightful and productive practicing requires 20% to 30% thoughtful silence. (For a strategy that requires even more silence, see Chapter 8, on imaging).

Heuristic thinking refers to the unconscious thought process that causes you to discover the solution to a problem without attending to it directly. Imagine, for example, that you have misplaced your keys. You look for them frantically all over the house, you try to remember the last time you had them, and so on. After searching desperately for a half hour, you give up and start doing other things. All of a sudden you realize where they are, and you are right. *Lateral thinking* is a term coined by Edward de Bono to describe creative thinking, or thinking outside the box. It refers to a system of thought that enables you to create solutions that are not part of your current perspective. To learn more about this type of thinking, go to de Bono's Web site, www.sixhats.com.

Inattention as Practice Power

It is common for a musician to try to fix the intonation, the tone, the rhythm, *and* the phrasing all at once, in a single practice session. Practically speaking, this may mean working on one measure of a piece for 20 minutes. Even if success is achieved after much practice today, often very little of that control is available the next day. This causes the musician to feel frustrated that the work is not building toward the eventual goal. This tendency to demand more than is reasonably manageable is likely also to lead to diminished concentration, as well as to self-deprecation and despair. The Rule of Selective Inattention protects against this avoidable misery by focusing the musician on a single aspect of her playing at a time. Just as one can be patient to the point of absurdity, tackling more than a person is capable of handling at one time can be overwhelming.

The Rule of Selective Inattention

The classic sign that your attention is overloaded is that your concentration diminishes although you are not fatigued. In addition, you may find that in spite of spending a great deal of time to improve a specific part, your work is not paying off. To improve your concentration, follow these steps:

Step 1 Play through the part on which you are working to observe which aspect of your playing is most out of balance (e.g., rhythm, intonation, tone, expression). Choose only one problem area and ignore the others. It is to your greatest advantage to concentrate on the problem that is most out of balance first. Once you've limited your attention to a manageable quantity, you can expect your powers of concentration to return.

Step 2 Beware the voice of your Interior Gremlin. You will still be able to notice the other aspects of the passage that need work, and your Interior Gremlin will try to seduce you to return your attention to them. Rather than pay attention to the demands of your Gremlin, focus more fully on the single aspect of your playing you've chosen to work on.

Step 3 When you have increased control over one aspect of the passage, stop paying attention to it and choose another aspect to focus on. Do not be disappointed or surprised if you lose some of the control you just gained while working on the first problem. Don't pay any attention to it; be *selectively inattentive*.

Step 4 Continue to cover each problem individually for 3 or 4 days (review "The Technique of Intimacy," Chapter 5, p. 39). As you continue to ignore all but one problem at a time, you will find that the individual aspects of the passage begin to come together by themselves. If they do not come together, at least you now have control of two or more aspects of the final product. Therefore, you stand a chance of integrating those items. It would have been impossible to integrate two or more items into a stable whole if you controlled only one of them.

Conclusion

I have always enjoyed paradoxes, so it is with great relish that I point out a way for inattention to improve concentration. As I pointed out earlier, concentration is your best friend even when it lets you down (see the Technique of Success at Any Cost, Chapter 5, p. 35). When concentration diminishes, it is a useful sign from within that you are demanding too much. The Rule of Selective Inattention is an appropriate corrective.

It is with equal pleasure that I present the impish idea that impatience can be good instead of evil. I shudder to think of a musician continuing to repeat a passage with hope in her heart through 5, 10, or 15 repetitions, even though there is no improvement. I am pleased to offer impatience as *a signal to seek a different solution*.

The virtue of both these strategies is that they enable the musician to make meaningful decisions from within without waiting for her coach to guide her. It is a blessing for the coach as well because the student arrives for a session in a healthier state of mind and body, with intelligent questions instead of the distress of inordinate frustration.

CHAPTER 7
Managing Your Daily Practice

One of the common dilemmas musicians often express to me is, "Even though I practice 4, 5, or 6 hours a day, I never seem to have enough time to cover everything." Since time is an obvious constraint in practicing, let's start here. The most obvious response to this dilemma is to reduce the amount of material you are trying to cover in the time you have available. When I suggest this, I am often told, "But that is what I was assigned," or "That is what I must prepare for the upcoming audition."

Each of these problems requires a different solution. Regarding your assignments, consider speaking to your teacher about the possibility of reducing the amount of material you are expected to prepare at any one time. One way to begin a meaningful dialogue with your teacher might be to reduce the load on your own and do a great job on the amount of music you know you can handle well. You can expect to receive praise for that part of your work, at least. Inevitably, the issue of how much you were assigned will come up, and you will have an opportunity to discuss the difficulty of covering everything assigned at the expected level of preparation. As for auditions, the Audition Time-Allocation Strategy presented in this chapter will give you the means to better manage your practice when preparing for an audition.

Improving as a Practice Manager

The Three-Day Practice Management Strategy

The Three-Day Practice Management Strategy will make you a more effective practice manager. An effective practice manager must possess several skills.

- He must be able to estimate accurately how much time it will take to fulfill a short-term daily goal to make an improvement.

- He must be able to organize the available daily practice time to cover a regimen of pieces and etudes.

- He must make plans from day to day that lead to fulfillment of long-term performance goals, including playing at lessons, playing for friends, playing a piece through for himself, and playing in formal performance spaces.

There is an exercise you can do on your own to acquire or sharpen these management skills and become a successful manager of your practice. It involves a Daily Practice Organizer (DPO) like the one in Figure 7-1.* If you follow the steps below for at least 72 hours, *exactly as prescribed*, you will learn a great deal about effective practice self-management. I cannot emphasize enough that you must adhere **strictly** to the demands of *each* step in this exercise if you expect to increase your management expertise.

The Three-Day Practice Management Strategy includes a number of procedures that may seem particularly draconian. The rationale for these unusual procedures is given after the following list of steps.

Equipment Needs: A timer that counts backward silently (a kitchen timer will do).

Step 1 Make your practice plan for tomorrow at the end of your last practice today. Start by filling in the total time you have available to practice tomorrow at the top of the DPO.

---

*The Daily Practice Organizer pictured in Figure 7-1 is a duplicate of an erasable plastic card that comes with my *Musician's Practice Log. The Musician's Practice Log* offers a system for organizing and keeping track of meaningful practice events over a 16-week interval. It helps the musician to identify his strengths and weaknesses and guides him to insights for improving his practice habits. The book can be ordered from www.magicmountainmusic.org.

Daily Practice Organizer

Total Time Available Today: _____ Hours _____ Minutes		
SUBTRACT 20% _____ HOURS _____ MINUTES		
Current Priorities: 1 _____ **2** _____ **3** _____		
ORDER OF PRACTICE (List each piece or exercise)	**AMOUNT OF TIME PLANNED**	**TYPE OF PRACTICING AND STRATEGIES PLANNED**
1.		
2.		

Figure 7-1 *Source:* Burton Kaplan, *The Musician's Practice Log,* Perception Development Techniques, 1985. The complete chart for copying is in the Appendix.

Step 2 Subtract 20% of that time. For example, if you have 5 hours available, you should subtract 1 hour, leaving 4 hours. Fill in the appropriate space at the top of the DPO.

Step 3 Now, list your current priorities at the top of the DPO. These are the items that you plan to practice daily over the course of the week, no matter what. Then, in the left column, list all the material (e.g., scales and arpeggios, etudes, pieces, excerpts) you plan to practice the next day. That list should include any stretching or other body care that is to be part of your daily regimen. Be sure that items 1, 2, and 3 at the top are your current priorities.

Step 4 In the right column, indicate what type of practicing you plan. Some examples of types of practicing that can be used separately or in combination are to maintain skill level, use rhythms to increase tempo, use the Technique of Intimacy to secure memory, use the Pie Strategy, simplify the problem, or model improved quality.

Step 5 Estimate how much time each task will take and write in the amount of time you plan to spend *on each item* in the center column. Do *not* include in your plan the 20% of time that you

subtracted from the total time available. In other words, you should plan *all* of your practice in *20% less time than you actually have available.*

Step 6 Tomorrow, *each time you begin to practice a new item*, set your timer to ring 5 minutes before the amount of time you allocated. When it rings, reset it for 5 more minutes. You now have 5 minutes to finish your work *on that item.*

Step 7 When the timer rings again, stop practicing and go on to the next item on your list, repeating the procedure in Step 6. You may feel that you don't want to stop when the timer rings. For the duration of the Three-Day Practice Management Strategy exercise, however, do not continue to practice the material after your allotted time is up. *If you do not stop when the timer rings, you will not benefit fully from this exercise.*

Note: Though you may not continue to practice an item once you have used up the time you planned for it, you *can* stop whenever you finish your work *in less time than you planned.*

Step 8 When you have finished all your planned practice for the day, you have 20% of the available time left to go back and finish other work you wish to complete, practice other things, or do whatever you like.

Step 9 *Make your plan for tomorrow at the end of your last practice today.* This is the moment when you will gain management insight if you followed all the steps above *exactly as prescribed*. When you make your plan for tomorrow, you should be evaluating the success of your time budgeting today. This awareness will improve your ability to estimate the time required to reach particular goals more appropriately in the future, thereby making you a more effective manager of your practice time.

How the Three-Day Practice Management Strategy Makes You a Better Manager

Each of the constraints of the Three-Day Practice Management Strategy is designed to improve a different aspect of management skill. The constraint that you practice each item for no more than the allotted time helps to develop your ability to make more realistic estimates of the time it takes to achieve each practice goal. When you make your plan for tomorrow's practice, you will have a realistic basis for improving your estimate and thereby become more efficient.

Most musicians find that they accomplish more in less time if they do not act as if they had endless time available. They also find that when they fulfill their practice time goals, they are less anxious and feel good that they have achieved their plan. In addition, this aspect of the strategy guarantees that you will have the time you need to practice all the items in your plan each day.

Another constraint is that you set the timer for 5 minutes less than the allotted time for each practice interval you have planned. Then you reset the timer for 5 minutes and stop when it rings again. This step is included so that you are not rudely interrupted right in the middle of your practice of an item. It allows you to estimate a comfortable conclusion to your practice of that item for today.

An additional constraint is that you plan to complete your practice in 20% less time than the total time available. The 20% of unstructured time avoids the pitfall of excessive regimentation. Less structured practice has several benefits: With 20% of free time

available at the end, you can go back to work further on items that need it. You can also reflect on the experience of the day of practice, make an improved plan for tomorrow, fulfill artistic urges by playing other works or sight-reading, and so on.

IMPORTANT: Keep in mind that the Three-Day Practice Management Strategy is *an exercise* in improving your management skills. Do not mistake it for the way you should always work. Keep in mind that this strategy will make you more effective as a practice manager ***only*** if you embrace it wholeheartedly, reserving your judgment of its value until you have completed the task ***strictly as prescribed.***

The Audition Time-Allocation Strategy

When you have an audition, you are often given so much music to prepare that it seems impossible to fit the work into even 6 hours of daily practice. Nevertheless, there is a strategy for organizing your practice to become more efficient with the time you have at your disposal. The steps of the Audition Time-Allocation Strategy will help you to manage your time as well as possible.

Step 1 Make a list of all the excerpts and solo repertoire required for the audition.

Step 2 Put each work into one of the following categories:

  a. Performance-ready or very close to performance-ready

  b. Not performance-ready now, but clearly possible to prepare in time for the audition

  c. Needing a great deal of work to be performance-ready, possibly more than time will allow

Step 3 In each category, rank the excerpts from most performance-ready to least performance-ready (e.g., 1, 2, 3, and so on, with the highest number representing the least performance-ready excerpts).

Step 4 Divide your time as follows:

• Apportion ample practice time for the works in category *c*. Begin with the least performance-ready piece first.

- Do maintenance practice of the works in category *a* (see "Maintaining Control of a Piece or Skill," Chapter 1).

- Allocate the remaining time to practice the works in category *b*.

Step 5 After you have made this list, ask yourself the following question: "Given the time I have left before the audition, do I have the time and the skill to practice the works in categories *b* and *c* to the level of the works in category *a*?" If you do, make your plans accordingly. If you do not, cancel the audition.

Conclusion to Part One

As the twenty-first century begins, neuroscience is advancing the frontier of knowledge about how the human brain and mind function. Much of what I have introduced in Part One is dependent on this knowledge. It makes perfect sense, then, that this type of knowledge about how we learn a skill is only now beginning to become part of music pedagogy. The possibilities of further exploration to refine the musician's capacity to empower herself in the practice room seem to be endless.

In Part One, armed with the new perspectives on how we function to learn a skill, we have redefined what constitutes practice, reviewed unproductive myths about practicing, become aware of the Third Hand as the ultimate source of musical control, and learned the techniques of the Basic Work Process. We have also seen the usefulness of impatience and inattention and learned the principles of effective practice management. When we apply our newly informed consciousness to a problem of music practice, we can now see ways to reorganize our behavior to achieve better results with less effort. If you combine the new knowledge and awareness you gained in Part One with instrumental practice strategies you already know, you can expect your practice to be more efficient and effective.

Part Two, "Practice Strategies for All Instrumentalists," offers numerous strategies to help you increase your technical and musical control. Some are refinements of time-tested strategies. Most of them are new strategies that address the thorniest problems of developing precision and consistency. There is the Imaging Strategy, which gives you a way to use your imagination to refine your playing ability. The Click Track Strategy helps you develop a reliable internal rhythmic pulse and connect it to your playing. The Strategy of the Vanishing Technique offers the gift of musical memory, and Super-Learning with the Rhythms Strategy enables you to develop accuracy in fast passages. Most importantly, numerous ways of using the metronome are introduced to bring you closer to expressing your musical thoughts and feelings. The adventure continues . . . .

PRACTICE STRATEGIES FOR ALL INSTRUMENTALISTS

I would like to take this opportunity to clarify the difference between the Techniques of the Basic Work Process and the instrumental strategies that are the focus of Part Two. The Techniques of the Basic Work Process are actually *self-management strategies.* They enable you to make decisions about how to choose the most effective instrumental strategy, when to switch from one strategy to another, when to use more than one strategy, when to repeat, when to stop improving, and so on.

Once you have decided on an aspect of work that needs improvement, you will always need an *instrumental strategy* to help you. The Technique of Success at Any Cost (Chapter 5, p. 35) requires you to employ instrumental strategies. The rules of the Technique of Success at Any Cost will help you gain the most benefit from the instrumental strategy you have chosen.

CHAPTER 8

Imaging: The Strategy of Strategies

It has become commonplace in the training of athletes to ask them to visualize new routines or amended routines in their "mind's eye" before they actually perform the routines. Effective visualization causes improvement in the real routine without actual physical practice.*

When I teach this strategy to musicians, I refer to the process as *imaging* rather than *visualizing* to emphasize that for the musician the image includes much more than the visual. In addition to seeing the notes and the body playing the notes (visual imaging), the musician must feel the body moving and touching the instrument (kinesthetic imaging). He also must hear the sound (auditory imaging) and experience the musical expression (emotional imaging). Many musicians report that this type of training has helped them increase their control, and articles in professional journals describe similar successes.† You may find it difficult, at first, to conceive of the word image as referring to a non-visual perception. Consider, however, how close the idea of imaging is to imagining. Can you imagine—*image*—the sound of a song you love, or the touch of a hand you shook, or the way it feels when you hold hands with your best friend? Whatever you experience internally when you imagine such perceptions is what I mean by an image, and *imaging is the process of forming the imagined experience in your mind*.

Creating the Image

The image you create must include the entire act of playing. *You should not have the instrument in your hand when you are imaging*. Your image should be as vivid, comprehensive, and detailed as possible.

You should see and feel all the playing parts of your body as they play the instrument. You should hear the sound. *The imaged sound should be an expressive interpretation of the written notation*, not merely rhythmically timed notes devoid of expression. Though it is possible to look at the music and image in this way, it is preferable to play from memory and image with your eyes closed. If you are playing from memory, try to see the notation in your "mind's eye."

The image you form should include what you see, hear, touch, and feel *as if you were actually playing*. In other words, you should not be looking at yourself as if you are taking a photograph from a distance, and you should not be listening to yourself as if you are sitting in the audience.

Irrespective of the particular instrument you play, your image should include the sound of your expressive interpretation and the feelings engendered by the imaged sound (both an auditory and an emotional image). If you play a bowed stringed instrument, you must also feel the hand in contact with the bow, feel the bow hair rub the string, see the direction in which the bow is moving, and feel and see your left arm, hand, and fingers perform their entire repertoire of functions (both a visual and a kinesthetic image). If you are a wind player, you must also feel your embouchure organized around the mouthpiece and feel and see your fingers depress and release the keys and cover and uncover the holes in the keys (both a visual and a kinesthetic image). To clarify further: If you are a clarinetist, while you are actually playing you cannot see some of your fingers and some of the keys. Nonetheless, you still form a combined visual-kinesthetic image in your mind of all your

---

*Mumford, Hall, "The Effects of Internal and External Imagery on Performing Figures in Figure Skating."
†Freymuth, "Mental Practice for Musicians."

fingers as well as the keys in order to play your instrument. Your image, therefore, is a composite of real perceptions and imaginatively constructed perceptions. Whatever instrument you play, experience all the necessary and appropriate auditory, visual, kinesthetic, and emotional details of playing.

Don't be surprised if one aspect of the image is weaker than another, *or not even present*. If that happens, take the time to try to improve the clarity of the part of the image that is inadequate. As the clarity increases, you will find that you play better. Be prepared for the possibility that clarifying the image may take considerable time and effort over many days.

Don't be surprised if your body misbehaves in your imaged playing. For example, a string player may mean to move the bow to the left or the right and find that, in the internal image, the bow bends over the string and the tip points toward the floor. A pianist may mean to put his fingers down on the keys at certain points in the music, but he might discover that in his image, his fingers lift off instead. All experiences of this kind are significant, and you will improve your playing by practicing to fix the image so that it matches what you hope to achieve when actually playing.

Imaging with the Metronomic Beat

So far the description of imaging is comparable to visualizing techniques as described in various articles.* Some years ago, however, I discovered by chance that if a musician tries to practice a difficult passage by imaging his playing with an actual metronomic beat as accompaniment, the control gained is far greater than if no metronome is used.

Why Does the Metronome Make Such a Difference?

Internal time is elusive. Our internal sense of time varies considerably with our mood, our level of excitement, our level of anxiety, and the mood and intensity of the musical experience. If the mood of a piece is tranquil, internal time slows down; if the mood is agitated, internal time speeds up. In addition, if we are agitated because we anticipate that we will not have enough time to achieve our practice goals, we experience time as speeding up. A metronomic beat serves as an *objective point of reference* to help us control the internal timing of our playing. Considering that the control of a musical instrument involves incredibly tiny micro-measurements of time, muscle movement, and auditory perception, the use of a metronome should certainly enhance the result.

In my experience, when musicians image a problematic passage without availing themselves of the metronome, they often fail to perceive problems in their internal image. After imaging the same passage *while using the metronome*, however, they invariably report that their internal image contains the same mistakes in the same places as when they actually played the passage. Musicians who use the metronome to achieve a more controlled, nuanced, and precise image are rewarded beyond their expectations. Remove the metronome, and the results are not even close. When you play a passage after having imaged it while using the metronome, you will be delighted to find that you can play it with less physical effort.

When Your Image Is Clear, You Are Ready to Practice

When the image of your playing is clear, image your entire practice routine. Do everything you would do following the steps of the Basic Work Process *in image only:* Observe and evaluate, use strategies to improve, define a goal, and stabilize your success. Be sure that your image contains all the sensory dimensions described above: auditory, visual, kinesthetic, and emotional.

The metronome should be used throughout the imaged practice, and you should maintain a very high standard of coordinating your image with the beat. When you can image the passage three times in a row satisfactorily, you are ready to try playing the passage in reality.

---

*Feltz and Landers, "The Effects of Mental Practice on Motor Skill Learning and Performance"; Martin and Hall, "Using Mental Imagery to Enhance Intrinsic Motivation"; Woolfolk et al., "Effects of Mental Rehearsal of Task Motor Activity and Mental Depiction of Task Outcome on Motor Skill Performance."

When You Play the Passage in Reality

As you play, "surf" the image of yourself playing, as if the image you have created is an ocean wave and your actual playing tries to follow the contour of that wave continuously. Consciously maintain the image in your mind as you actually play the instrument; act as if the real playing is secondary to *imaging* your playing.

Important Points to Keep in Mind When Imaging

- Do not physically hold your instrument while imaging.

- Do not move your body while imaging.

- Image with your eyes closed whenever possible.

- When using this strategy, you should expect to spend much more time imaging than playing.

- Do not always wait until your image is excellent before trying to integrate it into your actual playing. Switch frequently from imaging to playing. An interior dialogue will evolve as you switch back and forth between your internal image and your playing. This will help you to enhance and clarify both your image and your actual control.

Why Imaging Is the Strategy of Strategies

Early on in this book, I introduced the concept of the Third Hand. Imaging is the ultimate use of the Third Hand: You use your image to integrate all the components of playing an instrument into a coordinated whole, thereby making your body the obedient slave of your image. It is even possible to learn new pieces using imaging and then play them in reality with reasonable success the first time you try.

I have articulated the idea of the Third Hand to enable the musician to gain power over the imaging process, which gives us control over our behavior at all times. The imaging process functions continuously, both unconsciously and semiconsciously, in our everyday behavior.* It may be hard to accept the idea that your mind is working in your own best interest behind the scenes, unbeknownst to you. Consider, though, how often you make mental notes during the day to remind yourself to do everything from taking out the trash, to turning on your favorite program, to making a phone call. A mental note is an example of an image. As a musician, if you bring the imaging process to consciousness to clarify, identify, and experience its power directly, you will greatly increase your confidence in playing and performing. With it, you will expand your sense of your potential as well.

---

*To learn more about imaging in human behavior, read *The Image and Appearance of the Human Body,* by Paul Schilder, Wiley, 1935.

CHAPTER 9
Strategies for Most Occasions

This chapter describes a set of generic strategies for the use of all instrumentalists: Simplification, Isolation/Integration, Modeling, Inhibition, Comparison, and the Basic Metronome Strategy. No matter what problem you are trying to solve, you will want to use at least one generic strategy in conjunction with whatever more problem-specific strategies you have chosen. For example, one application of the Simplification Strategy is to practice at a slower tempo in order to observe and improve an aspect of the product that is out of control. Let's say you are trying to improve the rhythm in a phrase. Playing more slowly may give you more control of the rhythm and at the same time reveal moments when the rhythm is not steady. So you might use the Berry Strategy (Chapter 5, p. 33) to identify precisely how the rhythm is unsteady. And then you might decide to use the Rhythms Strategy (Chapter 11, p. 73) to improve the steadiness of the rhythm. This may seem trivial and obvious, but if you read the list of possible simplifications below, you will see that what is simple on the surface multiplies in its complexity as you develop your ability to manage your practice and refine your musical product.

The Simplification Strategy

The Simplification Strategy offers numerous ways to simplify a problem in order to establish an achievable goal without strain. It is often the first step in a multi-strategy approach to making an improvement in quality or consistency of control. The following simplifications apply to all instrumentalists.

- Change the tempo. In fast passages, you would necessarily make the tempo slower. Slow passages might also benefit from a change in tempo. Playing them faster might make it easier to experience the connection and flow in the phrase.

- Remove the rhythm; play only the pitches, but play them in an even rhythm.

- Remove the pitches; play only the rhythm.

- Design a better fingering.

- Decrease the quantity of material you're working on at any one time.

- Simplify the phrasing. Redesign the slur pattern. If the passage is slurred, play each note with a separate articulation. If each note in the passage is separately articulated, play them slurred.

- Lower the intensity of emotional expression. Play with 75%, 50%, or 25% of the full emotion you intend to incorporate in the performance.

- Sing the phrase; then play it trying to imitate the phrasing and emotional nuances of your voice.

- Without making sounds, finger the instrument as if playing the music, using the same rhythm and notes. Coordinate your playing actions with the metronome beat.

- Play without ornaments until the rhythm is established.

- Divide long notes into regularly articulated subdivisions (rather than sustaining them legato as written) to become aware of and express the rhythmic tension throughout the long note. This will create an awareness of how to express the long notes when you play them as written.

As you read the list above, it may occur to you that if you simplify the problem, it might take you longer to achieve the result. At first, using the Simplification Strategy in practice makes you *feel* as if time is passing slowly, as if you are losing ground. In reality, however, it is the shortest way. The alternative is to work for days and days, protecting yourself from painful frustration and hoping, without evidence, that your effort will pay off. Stepping back to an "easier" version of the passage will enable you to build confident reflexive behavior that, once stabilized, will lead you quickly to the final product. More importantly, your performance will reflect that stability in its accuracy and consistency. Simplification is a temporary detour that is guaranteed to yield success.

Other simplifications are specific to particular instruments.

Special simplifications for players of bowed string instruments:

- Shadow bow and sing the phrase.

- Finger the notes and shadow bow.

- Practice without vibrato.

- Practice pizzicato without the bow.

Special simplifications for keyboard players:

- Sing one voice and play the other.

- Play with one hand alone.

- Play without the pedal.

- Play the pedal with the bass line (or with the line to which the pedal is related).

- Play the rhythm of two hands and pedal (in contemporary music, often the rhythm of the pedal is independent of either hand, creating three rhythmic lines).

- Conduct with one hand and play with the other (to establish the pulse, or to learn difficult rhythms).

- Play a harmonic reduction in rhythm (to hear the harmony, but more importantly, to get to the correct hand position in time, as opposed to note-by-note movement).

- Play only the outer lines (soprano and bass).

- In octave-chordal passages, play octaves without the inner notes.

Special simplifications for wind and brass players:

- Transpose a passage that "lays badly" on the instrument into a key or octave where those specific technical difficulties are not present.

- Change a note/notes in the passage to remove difficult-to-execute intervals.

- Play the passage louder or softer to make the notes speak more easily.

- In extended passages in which the breathing is a challenge, count out the phrase while blowing into a breathing bag so as to see the rate of air expenditure over the duration of that phrase and budget accordingly.

- Count out the phrase while blowing a single note, imagining the actual phrase all the while.

- When the passage is extended to the point where breathing becomes a challenge, start near the end of the phrase, playing to the end in the dynamic and character intended. Then continue adding bits to the section, slowly "building the phrase from the back end."

- For brass players: "Buzz" the passage, attempting to maintain the appropriate rhythm, qualities of phrase and articulation, perhaps the exact pitches of the notes, or any combination of these components.

The Isolation-Integration Strategy

The Isolation-Integration Strategy is a way of ensuring that the improvements you make to separate pieces of a phrase are integrated seamlessly into the rhythmic flow of the *whole* phrase. It is common practice to isolate as little as one note to perfect its intonation or tonal inflection. Because small details are of great importance in musical expression, this might seem perfectly reasonable. However, this procedure has severe limitations. Musicians who isolate notes to improve them find that the improvements *do not hold* when they are reinserted into the larger phrase. The same difficulty often occurs when whole phrases are reinserted into large sections of a piece.

It's easy to understand how this can happen if we examine a similar event in a different activity. Let's say that you're a visual artist and you're drawing a portrait. You stand back to review the unfinished work and decide that the eyes you've drawn do not quite fit in the face as you've conceived it. You start painting with an idea in mind and work for 15 minutes on each eye so that they each seem exactly as you want them. You then stand back and are horrified to find that the eyes you drew, which are beautiful in themselves, don't fit in the face you've been drawing. In order to succeed in drawing eyes that fit in the face, you must step back frequently as you draw the eyes in order to observe the effect of the changes you are making on the face as a whole.*

Isolating a group of notes to perfect them is easier than playing the same group within the larger phrase. Each time you isolate a note or group of notes to perfect them, you have as much time as you need to prepare the improvement. You can stop, prepare for the improvement, try it, and stop afterward. When you put that group of notes back into the context of the larger phrase, however, you do not have the same luxury of time. You must coordinate your improvement within the continuity and rhythmic constraints of the ongoing beat. Therefore, after achieving control out of context, you will need an interim strategy that will enable you to weave the improved section back into the fabric of the larger work. The Isolation-Integration Strategy enables you to integrate the isolated group into the larger phrase:

Step 1 Repeat the isolated group of notes until you can play the improved version *successfully* three times in a row.

Step 2 Now, start playing one or two measures *before* the part you improved, and play to one or two measures *after* the previously improved passage, until that larger section is stable.

Step 3 Repeat this larger section until you can maintain its quality three times in a row.

Step 4 Now, integrate the larger section into the context of the entire phrase, working to experience a seamless integration of the isolated group in the phrase three times in a row.

Step 5 Repeat the entire phrase, including the seamlessly integrated group, until you can maintain its quality three times in a row.

Seamless integration means that **there are no external or internal hesitations in your playing.** An external hesitation is a glitch in the continuity of control that is obvious to the listener. An internal hesitation is a thought, such as "Phew! I made it" or "Uh-oh! Here comes that spot again where I always mess up." Though the internal glitch may not be apparent in your sound when you practice, it is an inherent instability, which is likely to become an *external* glitch in a real performance if it is ignored.

The Modeling Strategy

Modeling is the first step in raising the quality level of your intonation, rhythm, tone, or expression. It is a four-step process.

Step 1 Create a model of improved quality—tone, rhythm, intonation, or expression—on as small an amount of material as possible.

Step 2 Repeat the improved model in a rhythmic manner until it seems comfortable.

Step 3 When you are satisfied with your control of the model, do not stop repeating it. Segue into the passage in an attempt to play the entire passage with the improved quality. Stop the moment you lose control of the new quality.

Step 4 If you stop because you've lost control of the new quality, begin with Step 1 again.

To clarify, we'll apply these four steps to the tone quality of a sample passage (Figure 9-1).

Figure 9-1 *Source: Mozart,* Oboe Concerto in C major, *K314.*

*Perls et al., *Gestalt Therapy.*

Step 1 Model the tone using the first note of the passage without time constraints (Figure 9-2).

Figure 9-2

Step 2 When you have good control of the model, put it into a rhythmic time frame (Figure 9-3).

Figure 9-3

Step 3 Start as in Step 2. As you play the note in a slow-motion tempo, get ready to play the passage. When you feel ready, do not stop playing—segue into the passage (Figure 9-4). Stop playing the moment you lose control of the tone and go on to Step 4. If you maintain your model as you play the entire passage, repeat it now at least three times in a row to stabilize it.

"Whoops, I lost control."

Figure 9-4

Step 4 Start again from Step 1 to reestablish the model. Use the Rule of Impatience to guide you (i.e., if you fail to sustain the model three times in a row, stop and change your goal).

You can apply the Modeling Strategy to improve any aspect of the musical product: tone, intonation, rhythm, or expression.

The Inhibition Strategy

The Inhibition Strategy is used to correct poor coordination that is interfering with the smooth rhythmic flow of a phrase. Inhibition is something we often try to avoid. In the Alexander Technique, however, it is the first step in altering a habitual pattern of undesired behavior.* In order to play with a consistently high quality, you must chain together a series of coordinated muscle actions to produce a smooth and rhythmically organized series of sounds as musical gestures. If the continuous chain of muscle action breaks, you will likely lose control not only at the moment of the break, but in the notes that follow as well. Musicians often repeat these broken chains over and over, thus reinforcing their unsuccessful conditioning. Try the Inhibition Strategy instead.

Step 1 Stop at the first moment that there is a break or a glitch in the chain of movements (i.e., inhibit the continuation of the chain of movements).

Step 2 Repair the break or glitch in that spot.

Step 3 Start again, prepared in advance to produce a smooth and continuous chain of events at the point of the break or glitch ("forewarned is forearmed"). If after two or three tries you still cannot achieve this continuity, leave the Inhibition Strategy and consider using the Simplification Strategy at this juncture instead.

---

*F.M. Alexander devised a detailed technique to help people replace undesirable habitual postural behaviors with desirable ones. His technique has proved beneficial in improving the muscle efficacy of musicians and other performing artists. See also de Alcantara, *Indirect Procedures*.

The Comparison Strategy

When you cannot decide between two or more fingerings, bowings, phrase patterns, musical ideas, or the like, use the Comparison Strategy. It is a six-step process.

Step 1 Compare only two of all of the possible versions at a time.

Step 2 Play version #1 completely through; play version #2 completely through. It is essential that each of the two versions you are comparing be complete and played one after the other. Keep a written record of the result (e.g., "#1 better").

Step 3 Try the same comparison again until you have conducted *at least three trials*. If the result seems very close, reverse the order of the two versions. Write down the results. Accept the winner.

Step 4 If you have more than two versions to compare, you now compare the third one with the winner of the first comparison. Follow Steps 2 and 3 again.

Step 5 If you end up with a tie between two versions, two other considerations can help you establish a preference. First, be sure that you make your choice close to the final tempo because some versions become awkward or impossible at faster tempos. Second, the tone quality of some versions is more aesthetically satisfying at slower tempos.

Step 6 If you find that there really is no difference at all between one version and the other, even at the final tempo, flip a coin or go with your gut feeling. It is very unusual for this to happen. Remember that the worst path you can take is to sit on the fence and make no decision at all.

Frequently musicians report being stuck, unable to decide between two or more fingerings. This is a waste of time. The following illustrates the Comparison Strategy applied to making a decision about which fingering to choose.

Step 1 Compare only two fingerings at a time. If there are more than two to choose from and you have already practiced one for a day or more, use that one as the first of two to compare.

Step 2 Play the phrase or phraselet once with one fingering and once with the other fingering. Do not practice the fingerings in the midst of making your comparison. If you have to stop in the middle of one of your comparisons, start all over again. *It is essential that each of the two versions you are comparing be complete and played one after the other.* In addition, it is important to play an entire phrase or phraselet when making your decision, because control of a fingering is often affected by the larger context and the musical idea. Keep a written record of the result.

Step 3 Try the same comparison again until you have conducted at least three trials. If the result seems very close, reverse the playing order of your two alternatives. Write down the results. Accept the winner.

Step 4 If there were more than two alternatives to compare, you now compare the third one with the winner of the first comparison. Follow Steps 2 and 3 again. In making your decision, be particularly aware that, if the fingering you have already practiced is the weaker one, there can be no question that it is *not* the preferred one. After all, it had the benefit of rehearsal.

Step 5 If you conclude that the fingerings are equal, there is one other consideration that might help you differentiate one from the other. Many fingerings work well at a slow tempo but not so well at a faster tempo. To be sure you are making the best choice, you must play at or near the final tempo. The faster you play, the fewer options will facilitate your control. If you cannot play the entire phrase at the faster tempo, you should at least test the small amount that contains the fingerings in question.

Step 6 If you actually find that there is no difference at all between one fingering and the other, even at the final tempo, flip a coin or go with your gut feeling. It is very unusual for this to happen. Remember, however, that the worst path you can take is to sit on the fence and make no decision at all.

This method of comparison can be used in choosing instruments, bows and reeds, the choice of timbre for a passage, and so on. Always play small amounts of a work when making your comparisons.

The Basic Metronome Strategy

The electronic digital metronome, which is common today, has been widely available for only about 15 years. All the digital metronomes available today are capable of speeding up and slowing down at the rate of 1 beat per minute. Before 1990, however, all metronomes were calibrated in a different way, namely, 40, 42, 44, 46, 48, 50, 52, 54, 56, 58, 60, 63, 66, 69, 72, then by fours up to 120, then by sixes up to 160, and so on. This arithmetic progression had nothing to do with facilitating practice, yet many musicians were taught to use the metronome by changing their tempo one notch at a time. The problem with that strategy is that if you were playing ♫ at ♩ = 40 and you went up to ♫ at ♩ = 42, the difference in difficulty was trivial. If you were playing 𝅘𝅥𝅰 at ♩ = 40 and you went to 42, however, you would experience a significant change. But that consideration was not universally acknowledged.

In other words, the number of beats per minute by which you should increase your tempo depends on the number of notes you play per beat. Use the guidelines shown in Figure 9-5 to determine the increments by which to advance the metronome as you practice. When you follow these guidelines to increase your tempo, you should succeed three times in a row at each tempo before progressing to the next tempo.

You can find additional strategies to use the metronome to play well at fast tempos in Chapter 11 (p. 73).

Guide to increasing speed if you are playing ♫, 𝅘𝅥𝅯, or 𝅘𝅥𝅰 per beat*

- If you have mastered playing ♫ at ♩ = 40,

  skip to ♫ at ♩ = 60 to play faster,

  then to ♫ at ♩ = 80,

  and finally to ♫ at ♩ = 100.

- Once you reach ♫ at ♩ = 100, it is not comfortable to play only two notes per beat.

  Change the metronome beat to 50 and play 𝅘𝅥𝅯 at ♩ = 50.

- If you have mastered playing 𝅘𝅥𝅯 at ♩ = 50, skip to 𝅘𝅥𝅯 at ♩ = 60 to play faster.

  Then move the metronome up 10 counts at a time — 70, 80, 90, 100, 110, 120, 130, etc.

- Once you reach 𝅘𝅥𝅯 at ♩ = 140, you will probably find it more comfortable to play

  𝅘𝅥𝅰 at ♩ = 70. To play 𝅘𝅥𝅰 still faster, increase your tempo only 5 counts at a time.

Figure 9-5 (A)

*The metronome numbers in the guides above assume you are using a digital metronome. If you have the older version of the metronome, use numbers as close as possible to those indicated in the chart.

Guide to increasing speed if you are playing 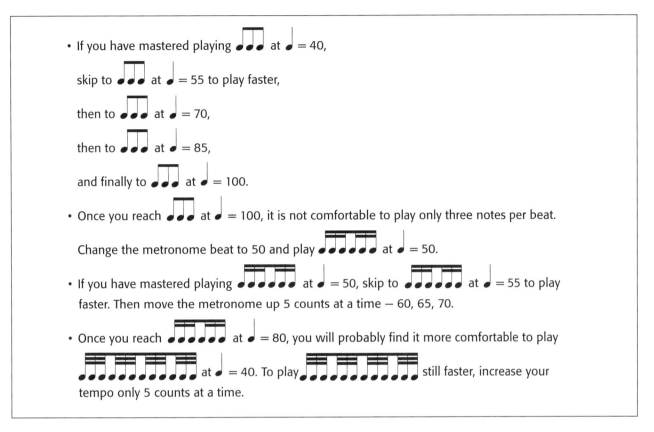, per beat

- If you have mastered playing ♪♪♪ at ♩ = 40,

  skip to ♪♪♪ at ♩ = 55 to play faster,

  then to ♪♪♪ at ♩ = 70,

  then to ♪♪♪ at ♩ = 85,

  and finally to ♪♪♪ at ♩ = 100.

- Once you reach ♪♪♪ at ♩ = 100, it is not comfortable to play only three notes per beat.

  Change the metronome beat to 50 and play ♪♪♪♪♪♪ at ♩ = 50.

- If you have mastered playing ♪♪♪♪♪♪ at ♩ = 50, skip to ♪♪♪♪♪♪ at ♩ = 55 to play faster. Then move the metronome up 5 counts at a time — 60, 65, 70.

- Once you reach ♪♪♪♪♪♪ at ♩ = 80, you will probably find it more comfortable to play ♪♪♪♪♪♪♪♪♪ at ♩ = 40. To play ♪♪♪♪♪♪♪♪♪ still faster, increase your tempo only 5 counts at a time.

Figure 9-5 (B)

Here are two questions I am frequently asked about the Basic Metronome Strategy and their answers.

Question: If I start slowly and increase the tempo progressively, must I start each day at the same slow tempo and work up to my fastest tempo? When may I just jump in at the faster tempo?

Answer: Musicians are imaginative and ambitious people. It is both justified and to your advantage to find out, when the spirit moves you, whether or not you have enough control to jump in closer to the desired tempo without going through the entire pattern of increasing your tempo from the slowest starting point. However, if your test fails twice within four tries (i.e., 50% success or less), back down to a slower tempo to work within your current limitations. The physical and mental strain that occurs when you try to play faster than your current level of comfort and control leads to an unreliable performance product.*

Question: How will I know when I am ready to try to play at a tempo closer to the final tempo?

Answer: As you work methodically from day to day as described above, you will be surprised one day to find that everything feels easier. You might try to go fast without warming up and succeed beyond your expectations. Beware of your desire to repeat this unexpected success. If you adjust your standard expectations to the level of your unexpected success, you are likely to be disappointed. Alone in your practice chamber, you may become "greedy" and fool yourself into thinking that you have greater control than is the case. If you pretend to yourself that your control is greater than it really is, you may even lose some of the control you have gained because your body will

---

*You will find meaningful advice about working within your current limitations in Jon Kabat-Zinn's *Wherever You Go, There You Are.*

tighten in its effort to act out an impossible fantasy. So keep in mind that control will happen when it happens and there's only so much you can do to help it. There is a very fine line, indeed, between imagining control and actually possessing it.

To review the guidelines for determining your tempo of control, reread "The Technique of Success at Any Cost," "The Technique of Intimacy," and "The Technique of the First Try," all in Chapter 5.

CHAPTER 10

The Click Track Strategy:
A New Way to Use the Metronome

The Click Track Strategy is a way to improve the objective accuracy and strength of your internal beat. If you find it hard to play in time—excellently—without a metronome, you would benefit from using the Click Track Strategy.

As musicians evolve into advanced players, they become increasingly adept at using the metronome to synchronize their playing with a regular, continuous beat. Unfortunately, when they play without the metronome, their control is often not as good. As a musician's sensitivity increases, he often makes minute corrections unconsciously when playing with a metronome. When the sound moves slightly out of alignment with the metronome's click (e.g., 1/50 second), the sensitive player tends to compensate very quickly without realizing it. He may think he is in control rhythmically, but he has actually learned to make these tiny adjustments so *it seems* that he is on the beat at every click. In other words, the metronome becomes a crutch. Without the metronome as a point of reference, the musician lacks the necessary precise internal control of the beat.

I developed the Click Track Strategy to enable the musician to expose any weakness in rhythmic control and to help develop a more accurate internal beat. Instead of using the metronome in the usual manner, in which each metronome click rep-resents one beat in a measure, you set the metronome to beat only once *per measure*. (Most metronomes cannot be set to a slow enough tempo to be useful in this way. For more information, see "Equipment Needs" at the end of this chapter.) At the same time, you set an unforgiving standard of playing precisely with the beat. The moment your playing is not perfectly coordinated with the beat, you stop playing, repeating the procedure until you've improved your control. The basic idea is to develop and follow *your* internal beat, not to depend on the metronomic beat.*

What, then, is the purpose of the metronome? To give you information (feedback) about the accuracy of your internal beat. It helps you determine if your internal beat is too slow, too fast, or metronomically precise. Once you know where and in what ways your timing lacks accuracy, you have a chance to improve it.

Using the Click Track Strategy

Step 1 Set the metronome to click every other beat; every measure; or every two, three, or four measures. (If your metronome cannot go slowly enough, read "Equipment Needs" later in this chapter.) In Figure 10-1, the metronome is set to click on the first beat of every other measure:

CLICK TRACK BEAT

Figure 10-1 Source: Brahms, *Symphony no. 4,* movement 3.

*Using the Click Track Strategy also enables you to experience more expressive room between click track beats than when the metronome is used in the usual way.

Deciding where to place the metronome's click depends on the tempo and the time signature of the music. For example, if you are playing in $\frac{2}{4}$ time and the smallest subdivision in the passage is an eighth note, you might want to set the metronome to click on the downbeat of every second measure, as in Figure 10-1. On the other hand, if you are in $\frac{4}{4}$ time at ♩ = 120 and the smallest subdivision is a sixteenth note, even one click every measure is already challenging.

Step 2 *Before* you start to play, **count each beat out loud** until you reach the third click track beat, as shown in Figure 10-2. Notice that you begin your count aloud saying "two," after the first click track beat has sounded. (The reason you don't count "one" at the start is because you don't know exactly when the first click will occur. Once the clicks have started, your spoken "two" expresses the length of the first beat.) Also notice that you begin to play at the same time that you say "one," out loud, on the third click track beat. If you are a wind player, do not say "one," just start to play.

Note: When you say "one" and begin to play, *continue to count mentally*—THINK the count— as you play. At all times, **stop** counting aloud or **stop** playing the instant you are not on the beat—do not try to catch up if you are behind the beat, and

do not slow down if you are ahead. Before you try again, take time to rehearse the passage in your mind with the click track beat, until it feels stable.

If you are a wind player and the music starts on a pick-up note, count aloud up to the beat before the beat that includes the pick-up, and then start to play as in Figure 10-3.

Step 3 If you cannot achieve complete accuracy, record your playing and listen to the recording to get ideas about changes you might make to coordinate with the beat.

The following rules will give you the maximum benefit from the Click Track Strategy.

Rules

Rule 1 Count with a snappy articulation, so that the words "one," "two," "three," and so on sound rhythmically crisp and precise. That will enable you to tell whether your voice actually landed precisely with the beat.

Rule 2 Your count should express the rhythmic stress pattern of the meter. In $\frac{4}{4}$ time, it should sound like this:

1   ₂   3   4   1

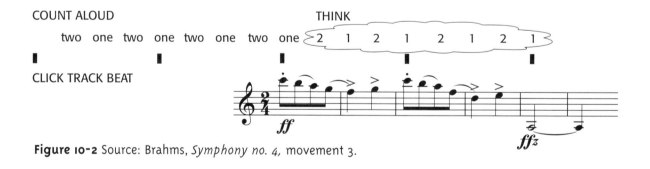

Figure 10-2 Source: Brahms, *Symphony no. 4,* movement 3.

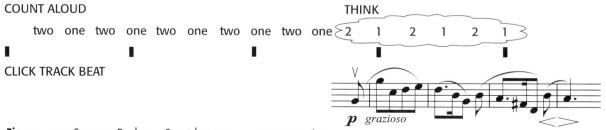

Figure 10-3 Source: Brahms, *Symphony no. 4,* movement 3.

In ¾ time, it should sound like this:

1 ₂ 3 1

Equipment Needs

In order to use the Click Track Strategy, you will often have to play at a metronome beat slower than 35. For example, if you are playing at ♩ = 120 in ¼ time, 1 beat per measure would be 𝅝 = 30. As of this writing, the best metronomes for this purpose that are currently available are Dr. Beat, models DB-66 and DB-88. To set the DB-66 model to beat 34 times per minute, adjust it as shown in Figure 10-4. To set the DB-66 model to beat 6 beats per minute, adjust it as shown in Figure 10-5.

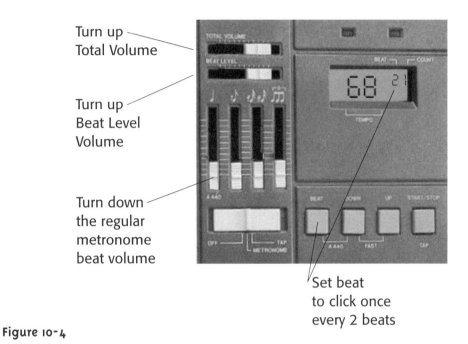

Turn up
Total Volume

Turn up
Beat Level
Volume

Turn down
the regular
metronome
beat volume

Set beat
to click once
every 2 beats

Figure 10-4

Turn up
Total Volume

Turn up
Beat Level
Volume

Turn down
the regular
metronome
beat volume

Set beat
to click once
every 6 beats

Figure 10-5

CHAPTER 11

The Rhythms Strategy and Super Learning: A Systematic Way to Increase Your Control at Fast Tempos

One sign of advancement in playing an instrument is the ability to play at fast tempos with good coordination. One type of passage that is particularly challenging for many musicians is a fast passage composed of repeated beats with the same subdivision, like the ones shown in Figure 11-1.

The Rhythms Strategy offers a way to master such passages. *Instead of playing the notes evenly, as written, you play them in different rhythmic configurations,* as shown in Figure 11-2.

Quadruplet passage from Rossini's *La Scala di Seta,* first oboe part

Triplet passage from Ravel's *Prelude to Le Tombeau de Couperin,* first oboe part

Figure 11-1

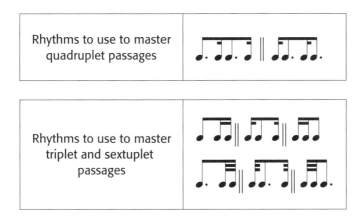

| Rhythms to use to master quadruplet passages | |
| Rhythms to use to master triplet and sextuplet passages | |

Figure 11-2

Figure 11-3 Source: Paganini, *Moto Perpetuo* (for violin and piano).

This use of rhythms has the immediate effect of improving the sequencing of the fingers so that the player puts the correct fingers down in the correct order. Once the finger sequence is stabilized, a major obstacle to playing fast is removed and the musician can usually play somewhat faster than before using the Rhythms Strategy. However, the final tempo may still be elusive.

Why Do Rhythms Help?

Two factors explain the control gained when using the rhythms strategy. For one, it is easy to move two fingers very quickly one after the other. During the time the player holds the long note of the rhythm, she has time to plan to move the next two notes much faster than needed to play the passage with continuous even notes in tempo. Therefore, the reflexes to trigger the finger muscles are being exercised at a rate faster than needed when playing evenly at the same tempo. Second, the Third Hand (the mind) is being organized to image patterns of notes and to coordinate the image with rapid finger reflexes. Figure 11-3 shows how the imaging mind coordinates with the fingers when using the Rhythms Strategy. While playing the long note ("play this")

you imagine the next two notes ("image this"). After playing the two rhythm variations shown in Figure 11-3, the player will have experienced super-fast movements between each pair of fingers.

Super-Learning with the Rhythms Strategy

It is not common practice to use the metronome when employing the Rhythms Strategy. However, by using the metronome in a rigorous and systematic way, it is possible to methodically increase consistent control at very fast tempos. I call this *super-learning*.

A unique relationship exists between the tempo at which you can play in rhythms and the tempo at which you can play evenly. This relationship is not intuitively obvious. The chart in Figure 11-4 expresses this relationship for four-note groups. Notice that each time you can play in the two rhythms shown— $\quad$ and $\quad$ —with the qualities described in the rules on page 76, you can expect to play even notes at a faster tempo than the tempo at which you played the two different rhythms. At Level I on the chart in Figure 11-4, playing in rhythms at $\quad = 40$, $\quad = 50$, and $\quad = 60$ gives

	When you can play in these rhythms: [♩. ♫♫ ♩.] & [♫♩. ♫♫.] at ♩= _____	You will be able to play [♫♫♫ quadruplet] evenly at ♩= _____
LEVEL I	[rhythm] & [rhythm] at ♩ = 40	[quadruplet] at ♩ = 50
	[rhythm] & [rhythm] at ♩ = 50	[quadruplet] at ♩ = 60
	[rhythm] & [rhythm] at ♩ = 60	[quadruplet] at ♩ = 72
LEVEL II	[rhythm] & [rhythm] at ♩ = 66	[quadruplet] at ♩ = 80
	[rhythm] & [rhythm] at ♩ = 72	[quadruplet] at ♩ = 92
	[rhythm] & [rhythm] at ♩ = 76-80	[quadruplet] at ♩ = 104-112
	[rhythm] & [rhythm] at ♩ = 84-88	[quadruplet] at ♩ = 120-126
	[rhythm] & [rhythm] at ♩ = 92-96	[quadruplet] at ♩ = 132
LEVEL III	[rhythm] & [rhythm] at ♩ = 100-104	[quadruplet] at ♩ = 138
	[rhythm] & [rhythm] at ♩ = 108-112	[quadruplet] at ♩ = 144-152
	[rhythm] & [rhythm] at ♩ = 116-120	[quadruplet] at ♩ = 160-168

Figure 11-4

your fingers a boost up to playing evenly at a tempo 10 metronome markings higher, namely, ♩ = 50, ♩ = 60, and ♩ = 72. At Levels II and III, the boost keeps increasing until playing in rhythms at ♩ = 120 makes it possible to play evenly at ♩ = 168. To be sure you understand it, study the chart in Figure 11-4 and the following steps and rules for super-learning using the Rhythms Strategy.

Developing Consistent Coordination at Increasingly Fast Tempos

Using the Rhythms Strategy for Continuous Four-Note Groups

The tempo relationships shown in Figure 11-4 are effective only for passages of continuous four-note groups, such as ♩♩♩♩ as well as ♫♫, ♬♬, and ♬♬. Notice that when you can play in rhythms at one tempo (column 1), you can play evenly at a faster tempo (across in column 2).

Step 1 Determine the maximum tempo at which you can play *evenly* with consistent control. Locate that tempo in column 1 on one of the charts (i.e., Figure 11-4 for quadruplets, and Figures 11-5, 11-6, and 11-7 for triplets and sextuplets).

Step 2 Practice the passage in rhythms at that tempo. You will achieve maximum control when playing in rhythms if *at the same time that you hold the long note*, you image the next fast notes (as shown in Figure 11-3). Your image should include the sounds you hope to hear **and** the finger actions needed to produce the next fast notes. If you are playing from memory, also try to image the written notes in your mind's eye.

Step 3 Practice until you can play the passage in each rhythm pattern three times in a row without any stops or hesitations, precisely with the metronome beat. Each time you stop, hesitate, or notice that you are not precisely with the beat, stop playing and rehearse the problem part until it is easy. Then reinsert it into context until you succeed three times in a row.

In addition, you must play in a musical manner, phrasing the notes, including dynamic changes, and including all slur patterns when you use the rhythm patterns. Many musicians have learned to remove all musicality when working on improving technique. This is not a good idea. While it is unnecessary to play with a full emotionality, it is necessary to play with some modicum of musicality. (This was first mentioned in the discussion of Myth 3 in Chapter 3, on p. 17. Return to it to refresh your memory.)

Step 4 When you can play the passage in each rhythm pattern with excellent control three times in a row, set the metronome to the tempo across in column 2. It will now be easy to play even notes at that tempo if you followed the rules below for super-learning well and maintained a high standard for accuracy and musicality. If it is not easy, most likely your quality standard, when you repeated the passage three times in a row, was not high enough. Try again tomorrow, aiming for greater precision and musicality when you play in rhythms. The key to super-learning using rhythms and a metronome is to *hold yourself to a very high standard for technical accuracy* **with** *a musical intention.*

Rules

Rule 1 When using rhythms, in addition to playing the passages as marked, practice separate-note passages slurred and slurred passages separate. If the passage contains mixtures of separate notes and slurs (like ♩♫♩), also practice those patterns in rhythms.

Rule 2 When you play in rhythms, play musically (i.e., include dynamics and phrasing).

Rule 3 Maintain a high quality standard for coordination, tone, intonation, and metronomically precise rhythm.

Rule 4 Do not move on to the next higher tempo for even notes until you can play each rhythm three times in a row at the standard you have set.

Rule 5 When playing separate notes in rhythms, sustain the sound, that is, do not staccato or spiccato. In other words, ♩. ♫. ♩ should sound like this: ♩.▬♩.▬♩ not like this: ♩₇♩♩₇♩.

Using the Rhythms Strategy for Continuous Three-Note and Six-Note Groups

The tempo relationships shown in Figure 11-5 are effective only for passages of continuous three-note groups such as ♫♩ (Figure 11-5) as well as ♫♫ and ♫♫♩. Notice that when you can play in rhythms at one tempo (column 1), you can play evenly at the faster tempo (across in column 2). Follow the preceding steps for super-learning when using the Rhythms Strategy for three-note groups.

Level I

When you can play in these rhythms: ♫♩, ♫♫♩ & ♫♫♩ at ♩ = _____	You will be able to play ♩♩♩ evenly at ♩ = _____
♫♩, ♫♫♩ & ♫♫♩ at ♩ = 50	♫♩ at ♩ = 65
♫♩, ♫♫♩ & ♫♫♩ at ♩ = 60	♫♩ at ♩ = 75
♫♩, ♫♫♩ & ♫♫♩ at ♩ = 70	♩♩♩ at ♩ = 85

Figure 11-5

Level II

When you can play in these rhythms:	You will be able to play ♪♫♫♪♪
♫♫♫♪, ♫♫♫♪ & ♫♫♫♪ at ♩ = _____	evenly at ♩ = _____
♫♫♫♪, ♫♫♫♪ & ♫♫♫♪ at ♩ = 40	♪♫♫♪♪ at ♩ = 50
♫♫♫♪, ♫♫♫♪ & ♫♫♫♪ at ♩ = 50	♪♫♫♪♪ at ♩ = 60
♫♫♫♪, ♫♫♫♪ & ♫♫♫♪ at ♩ = 60	♪♫♫♪♪ at ♩ = 70

Figure 11-6

Level III

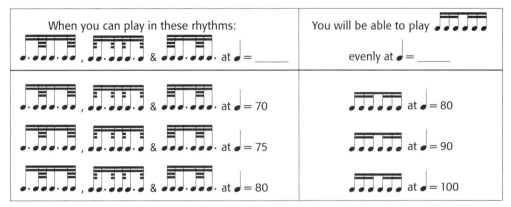

When you can play in these rhythms:	You will be able to play ♪♫♫♪♪
♫♫♫♪·, ♫♫♫♪· & ♫♫♫♪· at ♩· = _____	evenly at ♩· = _____
♫♫♫♪·, ♫♫♫♪· & ♫♫♫♪· at ♩· = 70	♪♫♫♪♪ at ♩· = 80
♫♫♫♪·, ♫♫♫♪· & ♫♫♫♪· at ♩· = 75	♪♫♫♪♪ at ♩· = 90
♫♫♫♪·, ♫♫♫♪· & ♫♫♫♪· at ♩· = 80	♪♫♫♪♪ at ♩· = 100

Figure 11-7

When You Can Play Triplets Faster, Change from Three-Note Groups to Six-Note Groups

If you are playing ♫♪ in rhythms and you try to exceed a tempo faster than ♩ = 70, you will experience significant strain to keep up with the beat. To exceed that tempo comfortably, start playing ♪♫♫♪♪ at a tempo of ♩ = 40. That would be the equivalent of playing ♫♪ in rhythms at a tempo of ♩ = 80, but it will produce less strain. The tempo relationships shown in Figures 11-6 and 11-7 are effective only for passages of continuous six-note groups, such as ♪♫♫♪♪, as well as ♫♫♫♪ and ♫♫♫♪♪. Notice that when you can play in rhythms at one tempo (column 1), you can play evenly at a faster tempo (across in column 2). Follow the steps for super-learning using the Rhythms Strategy (p. 75) for the six-note groups shown in Figures 11-6 and 11-7.

Super-Learning to Exceed Your Current Tempo Limit

Your current tempo limit is not the maximum speed at which you have ever played. It is the fastest speed that is always accessible without strain. At any time in a musician's development, there is a tempo that is the fastest she can sustain for a half-page of notes or more without any strain. That is her current tempo limit. Then there is the fastest she can play after working for 20 or more minutes, and the fastest she can sustain for short bursts of three or four beats. The super-learning strategy I have described will bring a musician to her current tempo limit in a reasonably short time. However, in order to bring her tempo limit to a higher plateau of control, she will need to apply a variation of the super-learning technique. The procedure is the same, but the payoff takes longer to achieve. For example, assume your current tempo for playing ♫♪ is

♩ = 132. To raise your tempo limit to ♩ = 138, it will be necessary to play ♫♫ in rhythms at ♩ = 100–104 for 4 to 6 days before it will be easy to play evenly at ♩ = 138.

This strategy to develop a new tempo limit is based on a simple idea. If you've never dived into water, how do you learn to dive? You put your head down and try to jump in head first. Will it be a wonderful experience? Of course not, but it's a start in the right direction.

Similarly, how will you ever play faster if you've never experienced playing faster? Somehow, the muscle must have the new experience. In the previous instance, the musician is trying to change her tempo limit from playing ♫♫ at ♩ = 132 to 138. If she only practices up to ♩ = 138, it will remain a strain for a long time. So she should begin to practice in short spurts at ♩ = 144 or 152. This strategy involves exceeding her goal tempo for a few beats at a time (see "Using the Add-a-Group Strategy," Chapter 13, p. 86).

It is important to try to spend 4 or 5 minutes working in this over-revved state. The consequence of spending that much time over-revved is that the muscle temporarily forgets its former limitations. It is as if it is hypnotized into a new state of capability, and it "believes" it can play faster. Now, if you slow down to ♩ = 138, it will feel easier, at least temporarily.

It is important to use this strategy with discretion because if you overdo it, you can strain your muscles. Practicing in this way a small amount each day will begin to build the new capacity gradually over several weeks. Without warning or trying, one day you will be playing faster and it will feel simple.

Do not TRY to make that happen. IT HAPPENS.

Multi-Note Rhythm Patterns

As the tempo is increased, the musician needs to be able to image increasingly larger groups of notes. This is accomplished by increasing the number of notes following each held note. Figure 11-8 shows rhythm patterns of more than two or three notes and their variations. As before, when you play the multi-note rhythm patterns in Figure 11-8 with the metronome, your ability to play even notes with an improved regularity and flow will increase. However, the tempo at which you can control even notes will be the same tempo at which you played the rhythm patterns—not faster, as it was in Figures 11-4 through 11-7.

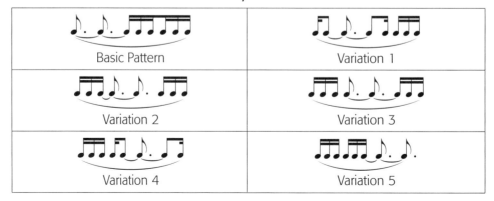

Figure 11-8

Eight-Note Rhythm Patterns

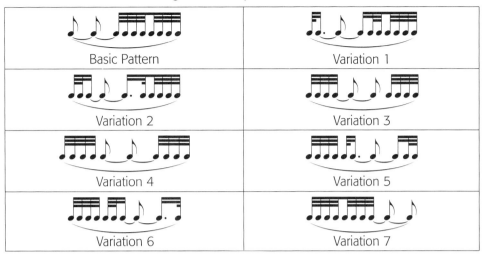

Figure 11-8

CHAPTER 12
Strategies for Improving Intonation

Factors of Intonation

Practicing to improve intonation takes an extraordinary amount of time. It is an aspect of playing a musical instrument that is a truly Sisyphean task. An anecdote about the famous violinist Fritz Kreisler reveals the demanding nature of intonation control. He was reported to have said, "If I don't practice for one day, I notice by the next day that my intonation is less accurate. If I don't practice for two days, the critics notice that my intonation is less accurate. If I don't practice for three days, the audience notices that my intonation is not accurate. . . . I'd better start practicing."

Like a chef honing a knife, the instrumentalist must sharpen his intonation control daily. But first, he must develop pitch sensitivity and control. Toward this end, musicians frequently employ amazingly counterproductive means in their practice. Many of these counterproductive efforts result from a lack of effective strategies for dealing with the challenge.

Controlling Intonation

Before you can expect to play consistently in tune you must be able to recognize instantaneously and accurately whether the note you are playing is in tune. If it is out of tune, you must be able to determine if it is too sharp or too flat, and to what degree.

It is also essential to understand that a pitch is not a single sound, but a complex mixture of overtones. If the pitch is not supported by a focused and resonant tone, one cannot determine accurately how in tune it is. Hence the word *intonation*, which refers to pitch as a state of tone. For that reason, a pianist can also be expected to influence intonation by the quality of tone he chooses to bring the pitch to life. The choices made in intoning each pitch in the context of the phrase help the listener to differentiate melodic from harmonic musical structure as well as to express the unique character of the music.

Most importantly, there is a hidden, usually unacknowledged factor that affects a musician's ability to control good intonation: *rhythm*. To produce any skilled movement, timing is the top priority. To play in tune, a musician must move the appropriate body parts so they are in the right place *at the right time*. A string player moves his fingers; a wind player alters his embouchure and moves his fingers; a pianist varies the touch of his fingers on the keys.

Fortunately, when playing rhythmically, timing is quite predictable. When you aim to be in tune on a particular beat or sub-beat within a steady rhythmic framework, you have a chance to control the intonation. However, if you practice slowly, without rhythmic direction, holding each note a different length of time to satisfy your priority to be 100% in tune, then the timing of your body's actions is removed from the rigorous rhythmic timing of the musical piece. Later, when you try to integrate your controlled intonation into the musical context, you will have to relearn how to play in tune in time (rhythmically).

What if, in order to play in tune, you must play so slowly that you no longer feel the musical rhythm, and each note appears to separate out of the musical pattern? Try the Note-Repetition Strategy to solve this problem.

The Note-Repetition Strategy

Sometimes it is more difficult to play musically in slow motion than it is to play faster. If, to control the intonation, the tempo at which you must play is so slow that you cannot experience the notes as a meaningful musical pattern, you need the Note-Repetition Strategy to succeed. *Instead of*

Example 1

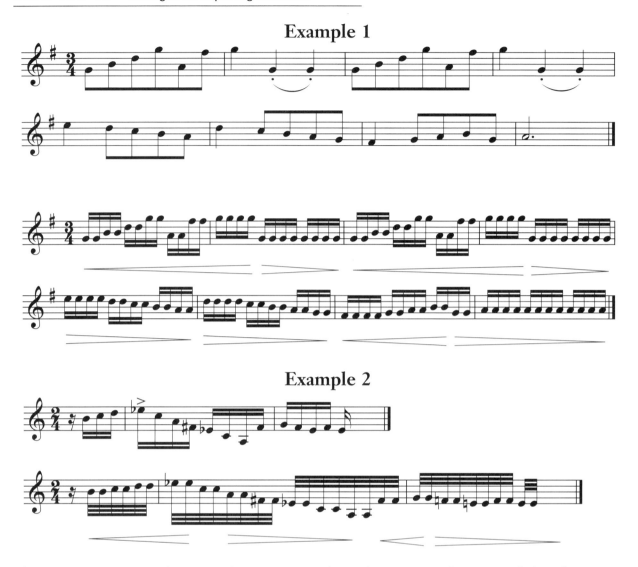

Example 2

Figure 12-1 *Source: Example 1, J.S. Bach,* Minuet; *Example 2, Schumann,* Symphony no. 2, *(scherzo).*

playing the phrase as written, double, triple, or quadruple each note while playing expressively. As you subdivide each note, you will experience rhythmic continuity, though each note lasts a long time. By phrasing the subdivided beat, you automatically aim each relevant body part in advance to play each successive note at a predictable musically phrased moment, as in the examples shown in Figure 12-1. Notice that your musical experience is more satisfying when you use this strategy. You will also find that the music does not feel as tediously slow as it did when you played it as written but in slow motion.

The Intonation-Pattern Strategy

Once you can play *musically and in tune* in slow motion with repeated notes, you still may have dif-

ficulty making the transition to play *musically and in tune* as written. Use the Intonation-Pattern Strategy to smooth the way to further control of intonation. Simply expressed, this strategy is based on the idea that *if one note in a group of notes is out of tune, the entire group is out of tune.* This may sound unreasonable, but consider: Once a musician can assess the intonation of individual notes instantaneously and has a good kinesthetic sense of the movements of his body to intone notes excellently, he has the further problem of coordinating a multitude of consecutive notes in tune within a continuous rhythmic beat.

If we were "hard-wired" to play a musical instrument the way we are hard-wired to talk, playing an instrument would be easy. We would simply imagine the intonation, and the relevant parts of our body would move with the same ease that our mouths move when we talk. However, the automatic links between thought and speech do not exist between thought and manipulating an instrument to make musical sounds. Instead, we must consciously organize and habituate our bodies to respond to our thoughts as reflexively as possible, so that merely imagining the music causes our bodies to move to create it. Therefore, we must understand how the body works in order to create and condition the most effective playing mechanism.

When you move one body part in any direction, other body parts move as if in reaction to the movement of that one part. For example, notice that if you reach your arm out to touch something, your head, neck, and shoulders also realign slightly. Your face and mouth muscles may even move, depending on the degree of motion of your arm and even more so on the degree of emotion that motivates you to move. (Take a moment to try it to determine the truth of this statement.) You can also observe this phenomenon if you watch your fingers move as you type. First, type one letter at a time. Notice that as soon as you depress any key, complementary movements occur in other fingers or in another part of the hand. Second, try typing a short sentence like, "Yes, I would like to eat something." When you are in the process of typing a word, you have an internal sensation of all the fingers preparing to type the word before you even move. As each finger goes down to type one of the letters of the word, the next finger is getting ready for the next letter. As a musician gets to know a piece of music and becomes aware of the note groupings he intends to communicate as musical gestures, he must train his fingers and all relevant body parts to move to create the note groups in the same regular, organized way they move to type a word.

One common strategy many musicians unconsciously use when trying to improve intonation is to stop when they hear an incorrect note, fix it, and then continue without repeating the entire pattern. This is of no value in learning to play the notes in tune the next time around because what has been learned is the entire interrupted event: Play out of tune, stop, correct the note, and continue to play the phrase. The next time around he can expect to play out of tune, stop, correct the note, and continue to play the phrase. There is no

memory of the correct *pattern* of notes. Another strategy is to linger a little longer on the note to adjust it as he continues to play. Then the musician continues, as if altering the rhythm when he lingers on the note is perfectly alright. The altered rhythm will inevitably be learned as part of the rhythm of the final product even though it is incorrect. Players who fall into these habits find that when they return to play the notes they have corrected repeatedly, they are still out of tune, or the music sounds stilted and hesitant.

The Intonation-Pattern Strategy guarantees an effective solution to this problem. You start from the premise that *if one or more notes in a pattern are out of tune, the entire pattern is out of tune.* You do not fix the intonation of individual notes. Follow Steps 1 to 6 below to use the Intonation-Pattern Strategy.

Step 1 When you hear that one or more notes in a group of notes is out of tune, stop playing. Decide if the out-of-tune notes were sharp or flat, and to what degree.

Step 2 Image the changed body movements in an attempt to play the entire pattern with the out-of-tune notes corrected in your mind. (For a detailed discussion of imaging, see Chapter 8).

Step 3 Now, actually play the pattern again, attempting to follow your corrected image as you play.

Step 4 Continue to repeat Steps 2 and 3 until you succeed through a process of trial and error.

Step 5 When you succeed once, try to repeat the corrected pattern at least three times in a row to reinforce your memory of the successful version.

Step 6 Now play the entire phrase with the corrected pattern, as described in "The Technique of Intimacy" (Chapter 5, p. 39).

It is important to mention another error in judgment musicians make when they practice to improve intonation. As failures accumulate, they tend to play slowly and carefully, so concerned that each note is correct that the rhythmic flow of the music breaks down. This creates a final product that expresses intonation but not music. As with words in a sentence when we speak, effective musical communication depends on integrating meaningfully inflected sub-patterns of notes (i.e., musical gestures) in the context of a phrase. It is the rhythmic organization of these patterns that creates musical sense, thereby compelling the audience to want to listen. (Reread "Controlling Intonation" earlier in this chapter to be sure that you understand the importance of rhythmic, musical control of intonation.)

CHAPTER 13

Increasing Control at Fast Tempos: The Add-a-Note and Add-a-Group Strategies

Creating music as you play an instrument involves a unique coordination of your cognitive and emotive capacities. On one hand, music as a compelling entertainment moves us and rewards us because of its emotionality: That is why we listen to it, and that is why we play it. At its best, music feels improvisatory to both performer and audience. On the other hand, music is composed of many redundant structures that must be meticulously organized and rigorously conditioned so as to be executed accurately. This aspect of music would seem completely opposed to improvised emotionality. It is fair to say that, for many musicians, a competition exists between the calculating, cognitive effort to control technique and the exuberant emotion they want to express.

This competition is particularly evident in fast passages. There appears to be a universal excitement experienced by both performer and audience when the music contains a series of very fast notes. This can easily get in the way of practicing to achieve control of the fast-note passages. Often, the musician gets so caught up in the emotional excitement of playing fast that his muscles tighten too much in an attempt to produce notes quickly. This makes it doubly difficult to learn how little effort is truly required to play fast. Playing fast notes actually requires less physical effort than playing slowly. This is not at all intuitively obvious to the player. It seems counterintuitive for the muscles to work less when the emotional excitement increases. It has been said that a performer needs to keep "a cool head and a hot heart." The Add-a-Note and Add-a-Group strategies show how to work on passages that require a calm body and mind in the context of a high level of musical excitement.

Using the Add-a-Note Strategy

The Add-a-Note Strategy is a way of organizing the sequencing of the fingers and producing confident, continuous finger actions with minimal effort. Phrases in virtuosic literature often end in a scale played *brillante*, like the examples in Figure 13-1.

Figure 13-1 (Top) *Source: Ziegeunerwiesen,* Sarasate *(for violin and piano).* (Bottom) *Source: Wieniawski,* Violin Concerto no. 2, *movement 3.*

Steps for Using the Add-a-Note Strategy

It is not necessary to use a metronome for the Add-a-Note Strategy, but do so if you find it useful. In the steps below, the Add-a-Note Strategy is shown applied to the first *brillante* passage (Ziegeunerwiesen) in Figure 13-1.

Step 1 Play the first two notes of a multi-note passage at a fast tempo—but not as fast as possible—and stop abruptly. Do not hold on to the last note you play. It should sound like the music shown in Figure 13-2.

Figure 13-2

Step 2 If you are satisfied that the first two notes are even and in tune, try to play them with less and less muscular effort. Put your arm(s) down and lift them lazily back to your instrument. This will relax the finger muscles. Repeat this procedure often to maintain the lazy muscular feeling throughout the Add-a-Note Strategy process.

Step 3 Repeat the group three times in a row with equal ease and quickness. Stop for at least one beat between each repetition, as shown in Figure 13-3.

Figure 13-3

Step 4 Now, add a note. Image the playing of the next larger group (i.e., 3 notes) before actu-

ally playing it. (If you are not sure how to image, read Chapter 8.) Repeat the new groups that are formed at least three times in a row with equal quality before adding another note, as you did in Step 3.

If you lose control when you add a note, start all over from the beginning (Step 1). As the groups get longer, you may want to add more beats between each repetition, as in Figure 13-4.

Step 5 When you can play the entire passage at a fast tempo with excellent control and repeat it without any trouble, change your tempo. Now play the first two notes *as fast as you can*. Continue to proceed from Step 2 to Step 4 and back again until you've completed the entire passage at the fastest possible tempo. Sometimes, you may reach a tempo that is faster than performance tempo. In that case slowing down to performance tempo will feel disarmingly comfortable.

Using the Add-a-Group Strategy

One reason to use the Add-a-Group Strategy is to build up endurance in repeating fast notes. It is based on the often-observed phenomenon that a musician who cannot play 4 measures of running sixteenth notes at a particular fast tempo may be able to play just 5 sixteenth notes at that tempo without any problem. Using a strategy similar to Add-a-Note, you can learn to sustain long lines of continuous fast notes at a fast tempo.

The Add-a-Group Strategy can be used to play slurred passages or passages of separate notes, such as the one in Figure 13-5. It can also be used to develop the ability to repeat the same note at a

Figure 13-4

Figure 13-5 Source: Schumann, *Symphony no. 2* (scherzo).

fast tempo for an extended period of time—a skill required from time to time on all instruments.

All the examples below show how to use the Add-a-Group Strategy to repeat sixteenth notes on one pitch for up to 20 consecutive beats, where a quarter note is one beat. The same process should be followed for passages with sequences of different pitches, like the one in Figure 13-5.

Steps for Using the Add-a-Group Strategy

Step 1 Pick a tempo to start that is on the border of "I can play this without difficulty" and "I am beginning to have difficulty sustaining the pitch for many consecutive beats at this tempo." For example:

- "My long-term goal is to play ♪♪♪♪ for 20 beats in a row at ♩ = 144."

- "Currently I have excellent control of ♪♪♪♪ at ♩ = 100. I can play 20 beats in a row evenly without any strain."

- "I begin to feel strain and slow down when I play ♪♪♪♪ at ♩ = 110. I can play for 3 beats before feeling strained and slowing down."

The next steps reveal how you can systematically progress from the comfortable tempo of playing ♪♪♪♪ at ♩ = 100 to the tempo at which you currently begin to experience strain when playing ♪♪♪♪ at ♩ = 110.

Step 2 Play one group with the metronome at the tempo where you begin to strain. Start from a note that falls on a beat, and stop on the note that falls on the next beat. The first group should always contain all the notes in one beat *plus* the first note of the next beat, as shown in Figure 13-6.

Figure 13-6

Figure 13-7 shows examples of other rhythmic note groups that can benefit from the Add-a-Group Strategy.

Figure 13-7

Note: For the purposes of this description, the rest of the examples given will be with sixteenth-note groups, but the same principles apply to groups of any size or note value.

Step 3 Play the first group three times in a row. Wait at least 4 beats between each repetition. It will sound like the music shown in Figure 13-8.

Step 4 Repeat Step 3, but reduce the number of beats between each repetition until there is only 1 beat, as shown in Figure 13-9, example "c."

Figure 13-8

a.

b.

c.

Figure 13-9

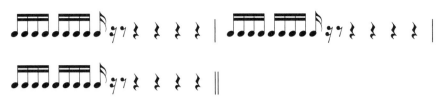

Figure 13-10

a. If you can play 7 consecutive ♩♪♪♪ groups without strain at ♩ = 120, like this:

b. but you cannot play 8 consecutive ♩♪♪♪ groups without strain at ♩ = 120,

c. then try playing 3 consecutive ♩♪♪♪ groups at ♩ = 130, like this:

Figure 13-11

Step 5 Image adding a group to be sure that you can conceive of the larger group in your mind. When your imaged playing is exactly in time with the metronome, play what you have imaged, as in Figure 13-10.

Each time you add a group, try to play it three times in a row with equal quality. *Each time*, wait at least 4 beats between each repetition, as in Figure 13-8, and *each time* progressively reduce to 1 beat the number of beats that you wait between each repetition, as in Figure 13-9.

Step 6 Continue to add groups until you begin to feel fatigue or you are not able to keep up with the metronome. Then begin the whole procedure again. If on the second, third, or fourth try you can go further, keep working. Otherwise, stop for today and try again tomorrow; or stop for now and try again an hour later.

It is not a good idea to strain your muscles past the first point of fatigue. *If you can control your eagerness* to develop your endurance at the new tempo today, you will find that within a week *your endurance will have grown considerably.*

Step 7 An additional strategy that can help you develop control at the faster tempo is to exceed the tempo at which you begin to feel strain in small spurts for 2 or 3 minutes. If you are playing triplets or sixteenth notes, add 10 to the current metronome tempo at which you begin to

feel strain to establish the next faster tempo. For example, if you have been able to get up to 6, 7, or 10 beats, but not yet up to 20, do some super-learning using 1, 2, or 3 groups at this extra-fast tempo for 2 to 3 minutes (see Chapter 11). Then return to the "slower" tempo. It will feel easier. Figure 13-11 shows an example.

Work like this for 3 to 5 minutes, and then try to play 8 or more ♩♪♪♪ groups at ♩ = 120 again. You will probably have increased the number of groups you can play without strain.

This type of training is similar to the training of weight lifters. If a weight lifter's maximum lift is 15 repetitions of 100 lb and she is trying to reach 120 lb, then some exercise is done at a still heavier weight, such as 3 to 5 repetitions of 130 or 140 lb. When the same weight lifter returns to 120 lb, she can lift it with greater ease.

Further Thoughts

Music is a dramatic art form. The humanistic psychologists, such as Abraham Maslow, describe music as one of the three peak experiences, food and sex being the other two. It is not surprising, therefore, that in using an instrument to create the transcendent effects made possible by music, the musician needs to experiment to find the boundaries of control. This means testing what appear to be limits to find out if they are true limits, as described in the last paragraph. We are too easily bound by the limits of the habits we have acquired over many years.

In the technical realm, experiment with a range of attitudes between carefulness and carelessness in your attempt to gain control of your instrument. Try out different degrees of muscle tension, from taut to flabby. Listen to the sound coming at you directly from your instrument, as well as the sound reflected back to you from the surfaces of the room you are in, and so on. In the expressive realm, experiment with how little effort can produce the loudest and fastest sounds and how much effort is required to control the quietest, slowest sounds. Investigate how gradually you can make a crescendo, diminuendo, acceleration, or ritard, and how abruptly you can produce these same effects. By granting yourself the freedom to explore your art in these ways, you will open the door to becoming an increasingly effective musical artist.

CHAPTER 14
Strategies for Memorizing Music

When musicians come to study with me to improve their memory, I always begin by pointing out how important forgetting is in human behavior. In each of our lives there have been events so unpleasant that memory of them would interfere with living comfortably in the present. I say this to make them laugh and to help them let go of the urgency they feel about memorizing music, a task at which they have often failed. When this experience of failure is present, musicians seem to despair of anyone ever helping them to be relieved of this burden. They are aware that for some, memory is easy, and they cannot understand why they have not been blessed in this way.

From Memory or by Heart?

Two expressions are most often used to convey the idea of memorization: "from memory" and "by heart." It is no accident that these two expressions are common ways of talking about the same phenomenon. They distinguish our ability to memorize abstract, even disconnected events and thoughts from our ability to memorize what is memorable because it affects our felt sense of the world. Likewise, music is a subject that can be learned as a set of organized movements to express the abstractly timed organization of notes as they are presented on the page. But it also can be learned as a deeply felt rhythmic organization of personalized sounds that have meaning on a level removed from academic discourse and from ordinary life.

Learning Music by Heart from the Start

In the "Learning New Repertoire" section of Chapter 1, I recommend that during the first two weeks of learning a new piece you should practice primarily to become aware of and express the meaningful musical gestures implied by the notation. In particular, you should identify and try to express the peaks and troughs of intensity in each phrase, as well as the emotional tone or mood of each section. During this process you will inevitably repeat phrases many times. When you repeat a phrase for the fourth time, try playing it by heart. But do not TRY to memorize the music; do not make memorization the primary goal of these repetitions. Your first concern should be to comprehend and express the meaning of the music. When you practice in this manner—by heart—you are using your short-term memory. It is like looking at an advertisement on TV or in a journal: 20 seconds after seeing it, you will have vivid recall of what you saw. If you try to access that memory 30 minutes later, much of it will have faded from your mind. After 24 hours it will have mostly disappeared, although there will still be traces of the memory left even then.

As you repeat this procedure daily, you will feel increasingly familiar with the music. Eventually it will become part of your long-term memory. It will simply become normal to play the music from memory, and yet you will not have consciously attended to the chore of memorizing it.

Memory and Meaningful Musical Gestures

Your memory will be enhanced if it is attached to organized musical structures. Keep in mind that a *measure* of music—though it is an identifiable substructure of a phrase—is not necessarily a musically meaningful gesture. If the gesture you're working on is musically meaningful, you're likely to remember it. The idea of musical gestures is discussed in Chapter 3 ("Isolate parts to improve them," p. 21). Return to that section to refresh your awareness of the difference between memorizing measures of music and memorizing musical gestures.

Distractions to Memory

Similar Passages Compete for Attention

Musical works often contain a number of passages that vary only slightly, and it's easy to confuse them—particularly in your memory. In fact it is quite usual for a phrase to return twice in a single section of a piece. Each phrase may be the same except for the endings, like A′ and A′′ in the piece shown in Figure 14-1.

In longer and more complex pieces, the same material may return four or more times in different keys and with slight rhythmic, melodic, or harmonic modifications. Imagine that you are memorizing a piece in which the theme appears with three different endings. Not only must you know each variation, but you must also remember the order in which the variations appear.

When you are confronted with this challenge, you can assign a number or symbol (e.g., A′, A′′, A′′′) to each of the similar phrases. Then put the symbols on chits of paper and mix them up on a table or in a bowl. Prepare three chits for each symbol. Pick one chit and play the version of the phrase it denotes. Continue to perform each phrase in the order dictated by your accidental choices. Then try to play through the piece in order (i.e., 1, 2, 3, or A′, A′′, A′′′), consciously directing the order of the similar phrases. When you eventually perform the piece, this preparation will serve to permanently clarify the relationship of these parts in your memory. If you have any lingering insecurity about playing the variations in proper order, you will be able to rely on your symbols to back up and organize your memory as you play.

Musette

Figure 14-1 *Source:* Musette, by J.S. Bach.

The Details versus the Whole

As musicians practice, they usually become aware of an extraordinary number of details in each phrase. For musicians who are accustomed to seeing the details as part of the whole, this is not a problem. For others, though, the details tend to obscure the whole. The musician confronted with a mess of details rather than a whole will find it difficult to memorize the piece.

In addition to details about the sound of the music, the musician is often thinking a great deal about how to move her body to produce the sound. Details of this kind can easily get in the way of memory. If you are overwhelmed by details in this way, use the following aphorism as a guide: "The phrase is the smallest meaningful unit of work."

This aphorism can help as follows: If each phrase is perceived as 15 details, then learning 5 phrases requires memorizing 75 details. Human memory cannot handle 75 individual items; the limit is 7, plus or minus 2.* However, by grouping 15 details into each phrase, you end up with only five phrases to remember—a manageable quantity. In books on memorization each phrase is referred to as a "chunk" and this memory technique is called "chunking." To increase your memory capacity, you reconceptualize relationships between small chunks so that each of 7 chunks—plus or minus 2—are perceived as one.

Negative Voices

After many years of practicing, a musician may develop a negative, judgmental persona that never leaves her practice room. Interior critical voices can be a distraction to memory, as well as to concentration in general. If you experience this type of distraction, there is a basic strategy you can use to help yourself disengage from your negative persona. The strategy may seem silly, but it is not nearly so silly as the voices with which you struggle. The moment you think thoughts like "You did it again," "You're really inept!" or Why don't you just give it up?" follow these steps:

Step 1 Stop playing.

Step 2 Put your instrument away in its case, and close the case.

Step 3 Speak out loud to your Interior Gremlin. "You just go over there and sit down. You're bothering me, and if you keep bothering me, I'm not going to keep playing until you stop." Elaborate this diatribe as you find necessary.

Step 4 When you feel ready, take your instrument out of the case and try again. Continue this procedure as often as you need to. It is likely that the voice(s) will stop for significant lengths of time.

Another strategy you may use to confront this dilemma is to write down every negative self-assessment as it occurs to you. Keep a piece of paper at hand when you practice, and each time a negative thought intrudes in your mind, interrupt your practice to write down the thought. If a thought recurs, you can use hatch marks after the first notation as shorthand to keep track of the frequency of the thought. If you find that these thoughts are chronic and pervasive, you may be able to stop them simply by putting your conscious attention on it.†

Unique Music Memory Strategies

The Strategy of the Vanishing Technique

The famous twentieth-century behavioral psychologist B.F. Skinner described a way of memorizing words that he called the "vanishing technique:"

Step 1 Write a stanza of a poem on the blackboard, such as this one, from W.B. Yeats' *The Lake Isle of Innisfree*:

I will arise and go now, and go to Innisfree,
And a small cabin build there, of clay and
wattles made:
Nine bean-rows will I have there, a hive for the
honey-bee,
And live alone in the bee-loud glade.

*Bruner, *Toward a Theory of Instruction*.
†Thanks to Scott Anderson, Principal Clarinet of the Honolulu Symphony, and Don Greene, well-known sports psychologist, for this technique.

Step 2 Read the poem aloud.

Step 3 Erase one word in each line and read it aloud again, still looking at it.

Step 4 Continue to repeat Step 3 until the entire poem is erased. You will be able to recite the poem even though it has "vanished." Do not be surprised, however, if you do not remember the entire poem tomorrow, as it is only in your short-term memory. (For a discussion of short-term and long-term memory, see "Technique Is Memory," Chapter 5, p. 39.)

I have designed a way for musicians to memorize music using a similar method. I call it the Strategy of the Vanishing Technique.

Step 1 Begin at the end of the piece* and using a pencil, bracket each phrase until you have outlined all the phrases in the piece.

Step 2 Cut out pieces of paper large enough to cover each complete line of music on the page and set them aside.

Step 3 Play the last phrase of the piece three times in a row *from the music* without any stop or hesitation.

Step 4 Cover the last musical gesture (or measue) of the last phrase, as in Figure 14-3, and play the same phrase—again looking at the music—three times in a row.

Step 5 Continue to cover one measure or one gesture at a time in the same way you did in Step 4 until you can play the entire covered phrase from memory three times in a row. If you lose control of your memory, immediately go back to Step 3 and start again. (Figure 14-4 shows the last two musical gestures covered.)

Step 6 When you have finished Step 5, back up one phrase. Play from the beginning of that phrase to the end of the piece—still keeping the last phrase covered—three times in a row.

Step 7 Work on the new phrase in the same way you worked on the last phrase, shuttling back and forth from Step 4 to Step 6, and always playing through to the end of the piece.

March

Figure 14-2 Source: *March,* by J.S. Bach.

Figure 14-3

*Why, you may ask, does the Strategy of the Vanishing Technique start at the end of a phrase and go to the beginning? Each successive phrase in a musical work is introduced by the phrase that precedes it. In order to play each phrase so the succeeding phrase has a sense of natural connection–*inevitability*, I call it–it must be informed by the phrase that follows it, as there is no other available motivation. You must know how the phrase will end in order to form the first part of the phrase so that the entire phrase makes sense. It is your awareness of the end of the phrase that gives you the insight into how to express the beginning of the phrase. Because memory is enhanced by meaning, the Strategy of the Vanishing Technique starts at the end of the piece to find motivation for each successive moment, thereby changing memory from an abstract task to a personal and organic one.

Figure 14-4

Step 8 When you have worked on at least three complete phrases that are now memorized as a chunk, you do not have to continue to play to the end of the piece each time you start work on a new phrase. Now treat the fourth phrase from the end as you treated the last phrase of the piece when you started this process, and memorize three more phrases in the same way. In other words, you'll be committing the whole piece to memory in three-phrase chunks.

Step 9 Each day, try to play from memory whatever you were able to play from memory the day before. If you succeed, play it three times in a row. If you fail, begin the entire procedure again. After four consecutive days working in this way, you will be able to play at least the music you played from memory the first day with security.

IMPORTANT: In order for the Strategy of the Vanishing Technique to work, it is critical that you adhere fanatically to one rule: Consider your memory flawed if you stop or hesitate while playing any part from memory. *Treat all stops and hesitations as **not memorized.***

Learn Simple Pieces from Memory

If you are an advanced player who has difficulty memorizing music, I advise you to build your confidence by memorizing simple songs first, in the following ways.

Obtain a book of simple songs that you have never played. Learn them from memory one at a time until you can play three or four songs in a row from memory. In the process of memorizing these songs, try all the strategies listed below:

- Learn to write out the song from memory.

- Visualize the written notation as you play the song from memory.

- Visualize the written notation and image the song at the same time.

- Once a song is memorized, play the same song in different keys without looking at the music, and play it in different registers on your instrument.

- If you have difficulty memorizing any phrase, try memorizing it from the end first, sub-gesture by sub-gesture, as described in the Strategy of the Vanishing Technique.

- Learn to memorize a song without ever playing it until you can image the entire act of playing it in your mind. Then play the song. Remember to keep the image you have created in your mind as you play it for the first time. Use the metronome while imaging, as described in Chapter 8.

When you have memorized 12 or more short songs using these strategies, advance to pieces of gradually increasing length.

Human Potential

If you are an advanced musician who has difficulty memorizing music, the following story can serve as a guide for what to expect should you try these strategies. A 30-year-old professional violinist complained that she had never, ever memorized a piece of music. When she came to study with me, she was already associate concertmaster of a good orchestra (one that paid a living wage). She had a large repertoire that included five concertos, such as the Tchaikovsky violin concerto, which she could play well only from the music. I immediately asked her if she could play "Twinkle, Twinkle Little Star." She laughed when she realized that she could.

She started to memorize simple songs, as described in the previous section. After two months of success, I asked her to begin to memorize the Tchaikovsky violin concerto using the Strategy of the Vanishing Technique. It took her 15 months to memorize the entire concerto. All the while she worked to memorize many other pieces of different lengths. After two years, she played the Tchaikovsky violin concerto from memory in an audition and won an even better orchestral position.

CHAPTER 15

Further Reflections on
Self-Empowerment and Practicing

I feel certain that if you use this book as prescribed, continually transforming understanding into doing, you will evolve a deeper and more fulfilling relationship to music. Musical artistry adds meaning to life—*and you do not have to be a professional musician to be a musical artist.*

I hope that I have demonstrated how conscious awareness offers musicians extraordinary power over their performing destinies. Keep in mind, however, that though consciousness is a tool that can enable musicians to reach further into their intuitive selves, intuition is an unconscious—or at best semiconscious—process. Intuition is nourished by consciously stepping outside the intuitive process to add new information. The intuitive process seems to struggle to digest the new conscious information until it finds an integral place within.

In Zen philosophy there is a metaphor for this transformation of consciousness into intuition: Before enlightenment a river is a river, a mountain is a mountain, and a tree is a tree. During the process of becoming enlightened, a river is no longer a river, a mountain is no longer a mountain, and a tree is no longer a tree. When enlightenment is achieved, a river is again a river, a mountain is again a mountain, and a tree is once again a tree. As you try out these techniques and strategies, for some time they may seem foreign ("a river is no longer a river"). One day, however, you will notice that you have integrated these formerly strange techniques into your practice, and as a result your intuitive, music-making self will have become enriched and empowered. I want to urge you to hang on during the awkward, transitional phase—your improved, confident, empowered musical self is coming.

Develop the Courage to Experiment

If you've worked through at least some of this book, I expect that you've improved the quality of your practice and enriched your experience as a musical artist through the use of your Third Hand. Do not be surprised, however, if you are still confronted with moments of frustration and despair. The most important advice I can offer to overcome that pain and hopelessness is to *experiment.* If you have an idea, no matter how strange, TRY IT! We musicians tend to be too afraid of making a mistake or of losing control as we try to perfect our technique. We need to take chances, both interpretatively and technically, and risk creating sounds we might end up concluding are the wrong sounds. We cannot be constrained by the incorrect versions we have already produced, and we cannot afford to adhere mindlessly to the advice of teachers and coaches if we expect to develop into artists. The advice I often give to help musicians free themselves of undue constraints comes from William Blake three centuries ago: "Excess is the road to the palace of wisdom. You cannot know what is enough until you know what is more than enough." Find out what is enough by experimenting; test the boundaries of what is possible.

Recalling the way we develop reflexive control of a skill ("The Technique of Intimacy," Chapter 5, p. 39), you have good reason to believe that an experimental approach on any single day cannot destabilize what you already have control of, since you will have only short-term memory of it. Therefore you will be able to successfully, effortlessly forget what did not work, certain in the knowledge that it will not compete with your existing habits, which are firmly lodged in long-term memory. On the other hand, you can also be certain that, no matter how well entrenched a habit is, you will be able to substitute an improved way of doing things if you so choose.

The song, "It's Second Nature to Her Now," from *My Fair Lady*, is testament to our capacity to learn our lessons so well that learned behavior feels and appears natural, or reflexive. What is exceptional in human nature, and of singular importance for musicians who are trying to improve, is that we can replace our current reflexive behavior—or second nature—with a new learned behavior that appears and feels equally natural. When we have achieved such a transformation, we might refer to it as our "third nature" or "fourth nature." This capacity is a tribute both to our extraordinary ability to remember and to our equally extraordinary ability to forget what was once second nature.

When you experiment with a new interpretation or a strategy for skill improvement, keep in mind that experiments do not often lead you to the exact outcome you were hoping for. That is the nature of experiments; they are based on hopeful guesses, or "guesstimates." Some might say that most experiments are bound to fail, but an experiment is only a failure if you judge yourself negatively for the result. I recommend a totally different attitude: Every experiment that fails to achieve the result you want is actually a *success*, because it leads to a more refined understanding of the challenge before you. The information gained from each "failure" narrows the field of possibilities. It is information in the form of, "Do not go in this direction; alter your course instead." I can guarantee you that if you cultivate a searching, investigative attitude to each experiment you try, you will be approaching a viable solution to your problem. You will be getting closer to the truth. Happily, each failure is information that clears the path to success—if you are courageous enough to see it that way.

Creative Interpretation: A Source of Technical Control

In this book, I have periodically referred to ideas about interpretation. I have referred to musical gestures (p. 91), to the distinction between musical rhythm and mechanical timing (pp. 17 and 19),

and to finding an emotional connection to the music (p. 26). Along with music practice, interpretation is a subject that has been left out of music pedagogy. In many parts of the world and in many teaching studios, the underlying instrumental philosophy is, "First learn how to play your instrument (gymnastically), then you can make music." Then, when you finally are deemed ready to make music, you are taught to imitate. The basic teaching strategy is, "Not like that, like this!" followed by the teacher's demonstration.

For years, then, the developing musician is starved from maturing as an independent musical artist. Then, when the musician-instrumentalist is finally deemed ready to become an expressive musical artist, there is a dearth of information about how to interpret the notation. For several centuries, music theory has been designed primarily to teach composers, not performers. There is no performer-based book that thoroughly describes the sound implied by musical notation.* Most musicians therefore lack the ability to perceive the dramatic implications of a musical score in the intuitive and expressive way they can read aloud in their native language. Moreover, I have found that it is actually possible to increase technical control by clarifying musical intention and integrating that intention into the practice process at a much earlier point than is normally done.

Toward that end, the next book in this series is planned to fill this void in music pedagogy. It will be called *From the Inside Out: The Musician's Guide to Personal and Creative Interpretation*. It will offer the musician-performer a new, systematic way to decode music notation to express compelling musical ideas and confidently evaluate their effectiveness—without a teacher. The book will also show you, the musician, how to increase your technical control through musical insight. And it will guide you through the process of organizing your imagination to produce the sort of compelling sound that undoubtedly drew you to play music in the first place.

---

*A few music theoreticians are working in this area, and foremost among them are Leonard B. Meyer and his one-time pupil, Eugene Narmour. Their books are listed in the Bibliography.

About the Author

Burton Kaplan is director of Magic Mountain Music Farm, where he conducts practice marathon retreats for 1- and 2-week intervals. He is professor of violin and viola at the Manhattan School of Music (MSM) and New York University. During his continuous 30-year tenure at MSM, he has taught the courses "Practicing for Artistic Success" and "Orchestral Excerpts" and conducted the Manhattan Chamber Symphony. In addition, he is director of Performance Power™, an organization dedicated to teaching a system for harnessing and integrating the powers of mind, body, and spirit in the practice room and on stage. In these capacities, he has influenced the growth of several thousand pre-professional and professional musicians.

As conductor and music director of both the Manhattan/Downeast Chamber Orchestra and the Empire State Youth Orchestra, he has performed at Carnegie Hall and Alice Tully Hall. These performances drew exceptional reviews: "Mr. Kaplan has fashioned the orchestra into a disciplined, precisely honed ensemble, one that plays with a crisp, biting attack and an obvious relish of making music in a vigorous, extroverted manner" (*New York Times*). In addition, under his direction the Manhattan/Downeast Chamber Orchestra has performed at the White House and won the American Symphony Orchestra League's National Youth Orchestra Competition. In 2000, he was the conductor of the All State Symphony Orchestra of the New York State School of Music Association.

For more than three decades, Mr. Kaplan has served on the faculties of the City University of New York and the State University of New York. He has also been Director of Education of the Downeast Chamber Music Center and the Third Street Music School Settlement in New York City. His career includes international appearances as a lecturer on instrumental pedagogy, sight-reading, and music practicing. He was the first instrumental teacher in the world to use video feedback in teaching (1967). He holds patents on devices for learning stringed instruments and a unique, tone-enhancing "shoulder horn" for violin and viola. Mr. Kaplan is the author of *The Complete Music Sight-Reader Series* (Perception Development Techniques, 1977–1980) and *The Musician's Practice Log* (Perception Development Techniques, 1985). He served as a member of the Cleveland Orchestra under George Szell and in the Pittsburgh and American Symphonies under William Steinberg and Leopold Stokowski. His solo performances were cited for "musicianship of a high order" and "extra (out of the ordinary) events" (*New York Herald Tribune*).

Appendix

Books Related to Music Practice

de Alcantara, Pedro, *Indirect Procedures: A Musician's Guide to the Alexander Technique*, Oxford University Press, 1997.

Balk, H. Wesley, *The Radiant Performer*, University of Minnesota Press, 1991.

Bernstein, Seymour, *With Your Own Two Hands*, Schirmer Books, 1981.

Bruser, Madeleine, *The Art of Practicing: A Guide to Making Music from the Heart*, Bell Tower Books, 1999.

Ericsson, K.A., *The Road to Excellence: The Acquisition of Expert Performance in the Arts and Sciences, Sports and Games*, Erlbaum, 1996.

Ericsson, K.A., and N. Charness, "Expert Performance: Its Structure and Acquisition," *American Psychologist*, 1994, 49(8):725–747.

Fletcher, Neville, and Thomas Rossing, *The Physics of Musical Instruments*, Springer-Verlag, 1991.

Freymuth, Malva, "Mental Practice for Musicians: Theory and Application," *Medical Problems of Performing Artists*, 1993, 8(4).

Gallwey, Timothy, *The Inner Game of Tennis*, Random House, 1974.

Gerle, Robert, *The Art of Practicing the Violin, with Useful Hints for All String Players*, Dantalion, 1983.

Greene, Don, *Fight Your Fear and Win*, Broadway Books, 2002.

Greene, Don, *Performance Success: Performing Your Best Under Pressure*, Routledge, 2001.

Herrigel, Eugen, *Zen in the Art of Archery*, Random House, 1981 (Pantheon Books, 1953).

Kabat-Zinn, Jon, *Wherever You Go, There You Are: Mindfulness Meditation in Everyday Life*, Hyperion, 1995.

Kaplan, Burton, *The Musician's Practice Log*, Perception Development Techniques, 1985.

Lieberman, Julie, *You Are Your Instrument*, Huiksi Music, 1992.

Loehr, James E., *The New Toughness Training for Sports*, Penguin Books, 1994.

Ristad, Eloise, *A Soprano on Her Head*, Real People Press, 1982.

Salmon, Paul G., and Robert G. Meyer, *Notes from the Green Room*, Lexington Books, 1992.

Thomas, Mark, Roberta Gary, and Thom Miles, *What Every Pianist Needs to Know About the Body*, GIA Publications, 2004.

Ungerleider, Steven, *Mental Training for Peak Performance*, St. Martin's Press, 1996.

Watkins, Cornelia, *Rosin Dust*, Cornelia Watkins, 9734 Railton, Houston, Texas, 77080, 2004.

Werner, Kenny, *Effortless Mastery*, Jamey Aebersold Jazz, Inc., 1996.

Bibliography

Aiello, Rita, *Musical Perceptions*, Oxford University Press, 1994.

Alexander, F.M., and Daniel McGowan, *Alexander Technique: Original Writings of F.M. Alexander: Constructive Conscious Control* (Abridged), Larson Publications, 1997.

de Bono, Edward, *Lateral Thinking: Creativity Step by Step*, Perennial Press, 1973.

Bruner, Jerome, *Toward a Theory of Instruction*, Belknap Press, 1974.

Caplan, Deborah, *Back Trouble*, Triad Publishing, 1987.

Conable, Barbara, *The Structures and Movement of Breathing: A Primer for Choirs and Choruses*, GIA Publications, 2000.

Damasio, Antonio, *Descartes' Error*, G.P. Putnam's Sons, 1994.

Damasio, Antonio, *The Feeling of What Happens*, Harcourt, 1999.

Dennett, Daniel C., *Consciousness Explained*, Little, Brown, 1991.

Deutsch, Diana, *The Psychology of Music*, Academic Press of Harcourt Brace Jovanovich, 1982.

Edwards, Betty, *Drawing on the Right Side of the Brain*, Simon and Schuster, 1989.

Feltz, D.L., and D.M. Landers, "The Effects of Mental Practice on Motor Skill Learning and Performance: A Meta-analysis," *Journal of Sports Psychology*, 1983, 5:25-57.

Goldberg, Elkhonon, *The Executive Brain*, Oxford University Press, 2001.

Goleman, Daniel, *Emotional Intelligence*, Bantam Books, 1995.

Johnson, George, *In the Palaces of Memory*, Knopf, 1991.

Kaplan, Burton, *A Point of View of Violin Teaching: Toward the Creation of a Method of Methods*, Perception Development Techniques, 1967.

Lederman, R.J., "Medical Treatmetn of Performance Anxiety: A Statement in Favor," Medical Problems of Performing Artists, 1999, 14(3):117-121.

Martin, K.A., and C.R. Hall, "Using Mental Imagery to Enhance Intrinsic Motivation," *Journal of Sport and Exercise Psychology*, 1995, 17(1):54–69.

Meyer, Leonard B., *Emotion and Meaning in Music*, University of Chicago Press, 1956.

Meyer, Leonard B., *Explaining Music*, University of Chicago Press, 1973.

Meyer, Leonard B., *Music, the Arts, and Ideas*, University of Chicago Press, 1967.

Mumford and Hall, "The Effects of Internal and External Imagery on Performing Figures in Figure Skating," *Canadian Journal of Sports Science*, 1985, 10:171–177.

Narmour, Eugene, *Beyond Schenkerism*, University of Chicago Press, 1977.

Perls, Frederick, Ralph Hefferlyne, and Paul Goodman, *Gestalt Therapy*, Dell, 1965.

Pinker, Steven, *The Language Instinct*, William Morrow, 1994.

Plaut, Eric A., "Psychotherapy of Performance Anxiety," *Medical Problems of Performing Artists*, 1988, 3:113–118.

Pruett, Kyle D., "Young Narcissus at the Music Stand: Developmental Perspectives from Embarrassment to Exhibitionism," *Medical Problems of Performing Artists*, 1988, 2:69–75.

Raffman, Diana, *Language, Music and Mind*, MIT Press, 1993.

Schilder, Paul, *The Image and Appearance of the Human Body*, Wiley, 1935.

Sloboda, John A., *The Musical Mind*, Oxford University Press, 1985.

Sternberg, Robert J.L., and John Kolligian, Jr. (Eds.), *Competence Considered*, Yale University Press, 1990.

Strogatz, Steven, *Sync*, Hyperion Books, 2003.

Todd, Mabel E., *The Thinking Body*, Dance Horizons, 1937.

Vygotsky, Lev, *Thought and Language*, MIT Press, 1986.

Walker, Matthew P., Tiffany Brakefield, Joshua Seidman, et al., "Sleep and the Time Course of Motor Skill Learning," *Learning and Memory*, 2003, 10:275.

Ward, "Musical Perception," in J.V. Tobias (Ed.), *Modern Auditory Theory*, Academic Press, 1970. This article is reprinted in T.D. Rossing (Ed.), *Musical Acoustics, Selected Reprints*, American Association of Physics Teachers, 1977.

Woolfolk, R., S. Murphy, D. Gottesfeld, and D. Aitken, "Effects of Mental Rehearsal of Task Motor Activity and Mental Depiction of Task Outcome on Motor Skill Performance," *Journal of Sports Psychology*, 1985, 7:191–197.

Success and Intimacy Collection Sheet

Piece, Movement, Etude _____

Quality and Goals	Day 1	Day 2	Day 3	Day 4	Day 5	Ideas

First-Try Chart

Piece or Movement _____

	AS PERFORMER			AS AUDIENCE	
Day	% of Success + Problems	Accept? Y/N	Day	% of Success + Problems	Accept? Y/N

Daily Practice Organizer

Total Time Available Today: _____ Hours _____ Minutes

SUBTRACT 20% _____ HOURS _____ MINUTES

Current Priorities: 1 _____ **2** _____ **3** _____

ORDER OF PRACTICE (List each piece or exercise)	AMOUNT OF TIME PLANNED	TYPE OF PRACTICING AND STRATEGIES PLANNED
1.		
2.		
3.		